C000052354

Cycle TOURS

Northumberland and Around Newcastle

Ted Liddle

First published in 2002 by
Philip's, a division of
Octopus Publishing Group Ltd
2-4 Heron Quays
London E14 4JP

First edition 2002
First impression 2002

Based on the original Ordnance Survey Cycle Tours series
first published by Philip's and Ordnance Survey®.

ISBN 0-540-08204-X

The route maps in this book are reproduced from
Ordnance Survey® Landranger® mapping.

Text and compilation copyright © Philip's 2002

This product includes mapping data licensed from Ordnance
Survey® with the permission of the Controller of Her Majesty's
Stationery Office. © Crown copyright 2002. All rights reserved.
Licence number 100011710

Photographic acknowledgements

AA Photo Library 27, 39, 45, 51, 57, 95, 99, 103, 107, 111 • Joe
Cornish 7, 63, 69 • Derek Forss 115 • Leslie Garland Picture
Library, (Leslie Garland) 91, (Phil Nixon) 87 • David Tarn 19, 33
• Jim Winkley 13, 75, 81

G Nicolson 17 IX 05

Contents

Abbreviations and symbols

Directions

L	left
R	right
LH	left-hand
RH	right-hand
SA	straight ahead or straight across
T-j	T-junction, a junction where you have to give way
X-roads	crossroads, a junction where you may or may not have to give way
'Placename 2'	words in quotation marks are those that appear on signposts; the numbers indicate distance in miles unless stated otherwise

Distance and grade

The number of drink bottles indicates the grade:

🍶 Easy

🍶🍶🍶 Moderate

🍶🍶🍶🍶🍶 Strenuous

The grade is based on the amount of climbing involved.

Refreshments

Pubs and teashops on or near the route are listed. The tankard 🍺 symbols indicate pubs particularly liked by the author.

Page diagrams

The page diagrams on the introductory pages show how the map pages have been laid out, how they overlap and if any inset maps have been used.

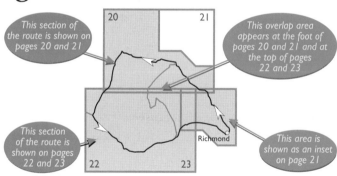

This section of the route is shown on pages 20 and 21

This overlap area appears at the foot of pages 20 and 21 and at the top of pages 22 and 23

This section of the route is shown on pages 22 and 23

This area is shown as an inset on page 21

Richmond

Cross-profiles

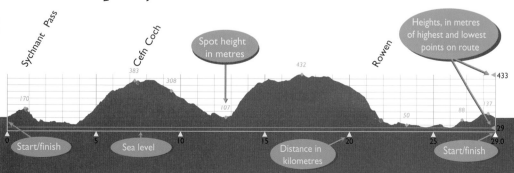

Sychnant Pass

Cefn Coch

Spot height in metres

Rowen

Heights, in metres of highest and lowest points on route

Start/finish

Sea level

Distance in kilometres

Start/finish

Legend to 1:50 000 maps

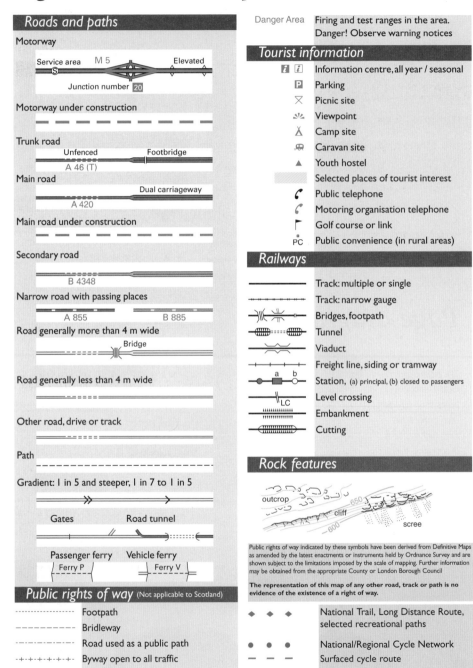

Roads and paths

Motorway

Service area — S
M 5
Elevated
Junction number 20

Motorway under construction

Trunk road

Unfenced — A 46 (T) — Footbridge

Main road

Dual carriageway
A 420

Main road under construction

Secondary road

B 4348

Narrow road with passing places

A 855 — B 885

Road generally more than 4 m wide

Bridge

Road generally less than 4 m wide

Other road, drive or track

Path

Gradient: 1 in 5 and steeper, 1 in 7 to 1 in 5

Gates — Road tunnel

Passenger ferry — Vehicle ferry
Ferry P — Ferry V

Public rights of way (Not applicable to Scotland)

.... Footpath
– – – – – – – Bridleway
–·–·–·–·– Road used as a public path
-+-+-+-+-+- Byway open to all traffic

Danger Area — Firing and test ranges in the area. Danger! Observe warning notices

Tourist information

🅸	ⓘ	Information centre, all year / seasonal
🅿		Parking
✕		Picnic site
℠		Viewpoint
Å		Camp site
⛺		Caravan site
▲		Youth hostel
▨		Selected places of tourist interest
☏		Public telephone
☏		Motoring organisation telephone
⌐		Golf course or link
PC		Public convenience (in rural areas)

Railways

Track: multiple or single
Track: narrow gauge
Bridges, footpath
Tunnel
Viaduct
Freight line, siding or tramway
Station, (a) principal, (b) closed to passengers
Level crossing — LC
Embankment
Cutting

Rock features

outcrop — cliff — 650 — 600 — scree

Public rights of way indicated by these symbols have been derived from Definitive Maps as amended by the latest enactments or instruments held by Ordnance Survey and are shown subject to the limitations imposed by the scale of mapping. Further information may be obtained from the appropriate County or London Borough Council

The representation of this map of any other road, track or path is no evidence of the existence of a right of way.

◆ ◆ ◆ National Trail, Long Distance Route, selected recreational paths

● ● ● National/Regional Cycle Network

– – – Surfaced cycle route

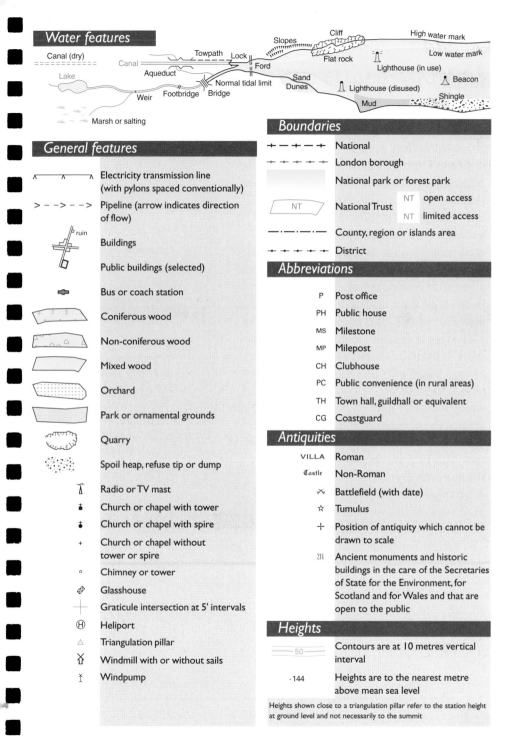

Water features

Canal (dry)

Canal

Towpath

Lock

Ford

Aqueduct

Normal tidal limit

Lake

Weir

Footbridge

Bridge

Marsh or salting

Slopes

Cliff

High water mark

Flat rock

Low water mark

Lighthouse (in use)

Sand Dunes

Beacon

Lighthouse (disused)

Shingle

Mud

General features

Electricity transmission line
(with pylons spaced conventionally)

Pipeline (arrow indicates direction
of flow)

Buildings

Public buildings (selected)

Bus or coach station

Coniferous wood

Non-coniferous wood

Mixed wood

Orchard

Park or ornamental grounds

Quarry

Spoil heap, refuse tip or dump

Radio or TV mast

Church or chapel with tower

Church or chapel with spire

Church or chapel without
tower or spire

Chimney or tower

Glasshouse

Graticule intersection at 5' intervals

Heliport

Triangulation pillar

Windmill with or without sails

Windpump

Boundaries

National

London borough

National park or forest park

NT   National Trust

NT   open access

NT   limited access

County, region or islands area

District

Abbreviations

P	Post office
PH	Public house
MS	Milestone
MP	Milepost
CH	Clubhouse
PC	Public convenience (in rural areas)
TH	Town hall, guildhall or equivalent
CG	Coastguard

Antiquities

VILLA	Roman
Castle	Non-Roman
⚔	Battlefield (with date)
☆	Tumulus
+	Position of antiquity which cannot be drawn to scale
⅏	Ancient monuments and historic buildings in the care of the Secretaries of State for the Environment, for Scotland and for Wales and that are open to the public

Heights

50   Contours are at 10 metres vertical
interval

·144   Heights are to the nearest metre
above mean sea level

Heights shown close to a triangulation pillar refer to the station height
at ground level and not necessarily to the summit

West from Durham City into the Deerness Valley

*T*his ride offers a number of interesting options. Three of County Durham's railway paths intersect near Broompark at a point that is only 2 km (1¼ miles) from the centre of Durham City. These paths are suitable and recommended for all but racing cycles and, as they follow the valley floor, they avoid a number of hills that the all-tarmac route cannot avoid. Several sections of level, traffic-free cycle path are possible on this ride, though there is a perfectly acceptable on-road alternative (with hills). The choice is yours. Valleys always mean hills but this route cleverly misses most of the heavy hills with one exception. The eastern third passes through several ex-mining communities with ordered rows of terraced houses with their neat and tidy gardens. The open road is soon attained and the route zigzags westwards along quiet roads that wend their way across very pleasant undulating countryside. At Salter's Gate, there are fine views of the North Pennines. The return route takes in the Lanchester Valley.

Start

Broompark Picnic Area, off the B6302 southwest of Durham City (GR 252416)

P As above

Distance and grade

54 km (34 miles) – plenty of short cuts but some have hills

///// Moderate

///// Moderate/ strenuous on-road alternative

Terrain

Generally undulating with one short brute of a hill between Low and High Hedleyhope – not a long walk/push. The on-road option has a steady climb south of Lanchester. There are a number of long downhills. Highest

point – Salter's Gate
350 m (1148 ft).
Lowest point – near
the start 62 m (204 ft)

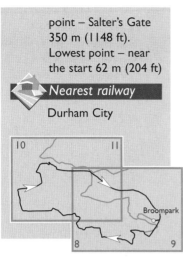

Lanchester 10

Takes its name from a nearby Roman
fort built on Dere Street, which ran
between York and Hadrian's Wall. Now
an attractive small town with a village
feel to it

Bearpark 11

Close to the Lanchester Valley Walk
across the River Browney are the
remains of Beaurepaire, which was the
monks' retreat from the monastery of
Durham from which Bearpark takes
its name

Langley Park 11

Product of coal
mining sometimes
used in TV and
film dramas.
Purpose-built
handball wall next
to the path
beside a row of
miner's cottages.
This was a
popular game in
the mining villages
of Durham

◀ North Pennines,
south of Edmund

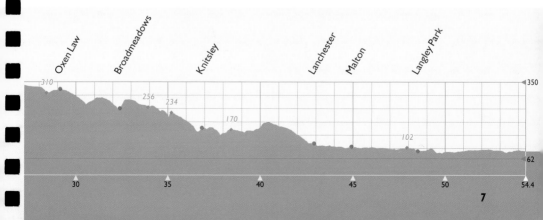

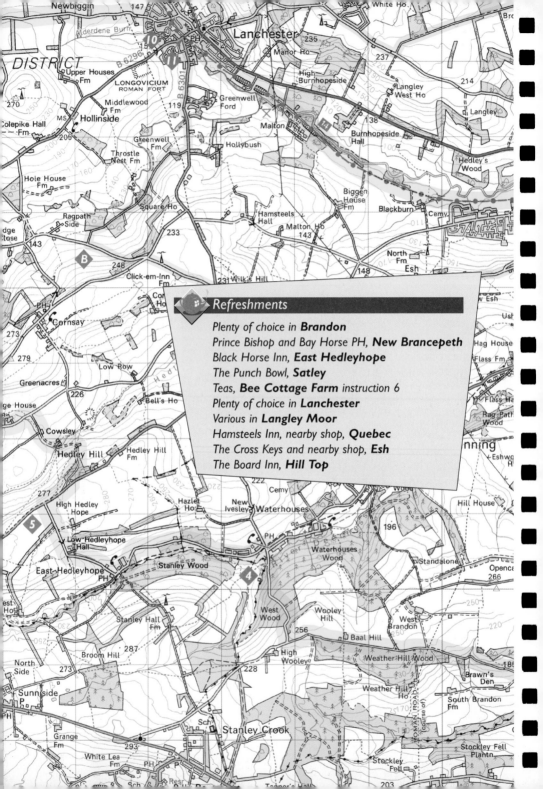

Refreshments

Plenty of choice in **Brandon**
Prince Bishop and Bay Horse PH, **New Brancepeth**
Black Horse Inn, **East Hedleyhope**
The Punch Bowl, **Satley**
Teas, **Bee Cottage Farm** *instruction 6*
Plenty of choice in **Lanchester**
Various in **Langley Moor**
Hamsteels Inn, nearby shop, **Quebec**
The Cross Keys and nearby shop, **Esh**
The Board Inn, **Hill Top**

1 Join the railway path, turn L. Bear R at path fork 'Brandon, Bishop Auckland'. Cross River Deerness (bridge – short push). Cross 3 roads, then turn R at next T-j to New Brancepeth

2 Turn L 'Pit House 1, New Brancepeth 1½', SA at next T-j. At hill top turn L (downhill)

3 Turn R for 4 km (2½ miles), turn R (NS) downhill to cross ri

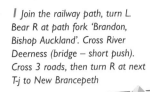

Alternative route

A At Langley Hall Farm turn L, then 1st R to T-j (NS). 1 km (¾ mile) steady climb to T-j, turn R (to instruction 2)

➡ **two pages**

4 1st L after crossing Deerness Valley Walk 'East Hedleyhope'. Keep Ivesley Cottages on R. Road bears R to steep hill – what you see is what you get! Levels to B6301

5 Turn R, then L after 400 m (¼ mile) down steep hill to T-j (NS). Turn L to X-roads SA to B6296 (**Or** turn R to Satley PH/phone). Turn L, then 2nd R 'Drover House 1, Salter's Gate 2½'

➡ **next page**

10 Before Main Street, turn R onto Lanchester Valley Walk at 'P Free' sign

11 5½ km (3½ miles) to Langley Park, then the same to 3 paths junction of instruction 1. Turn R to start (**Or** previous L to Durham City)

9

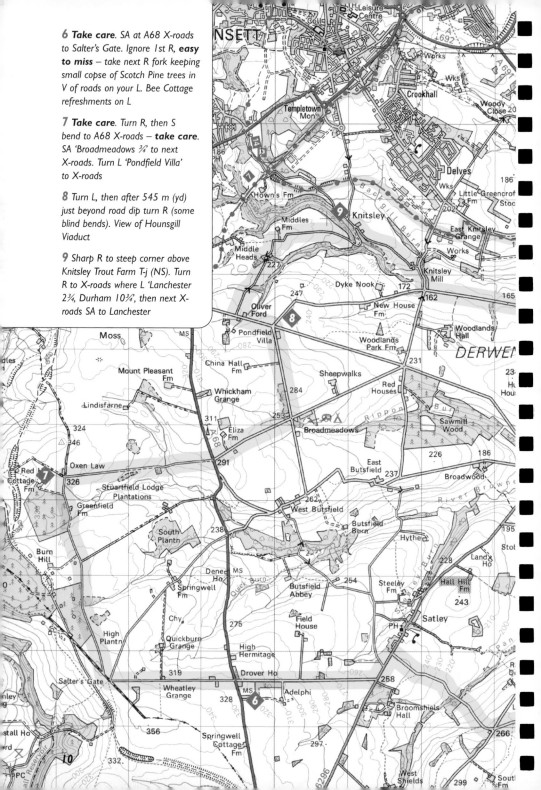

6 *Take care*. SA at A68 X-roads to Salter's Gate. Ignore 1st R, **easy to miss** – take next R fork keeping small copse of Scotch Pine trees in V of roads on your L. Bee Cottage refreshments on L

7 *Take care*. Turn R, then S bend to A68 X-roads – **take care**. SA 'Broadmeadows ¾' to next X-roads. Turn L 'Pondfield Villa' to X-roads

8 Turn L, then after 545 m (yd) just beyond road dip turn R (some blind bends). View of Hounsgill Viaduct

9 Sharp R to steep corner above Knitsley Trout Farm T-j (NS). Turn R to X-roads where L 'Lanchester 2¾, Durham 10¾', then next X-roads SA to Lanchester

10 Before Main Street, turn R onto Lanchester Valley Walk at 'P Free' sign

11 5½ km (3½ miles) to Langley Park, then same to 3 paths junction of instruction 1. Turn R to start (**Or** previous L to Durham City)

Alternative route

11 Turn next L after Lanchester Valley Walk (Ford Road) B6301 for 1 km (¾ mile). Turn R for almost 2½ km (1½ miles) to T-j 'Greenwell Farm' **NB** this is a county road

B Turn L, ascend to off-set X-roads. SA to B6301 X-roads. SA to Quebec and on to Esh. SA to Hill Top 'Bearpark 1½, Durham 4' (twice)

C ⬅ **two pages** At Board Inn sign bear R; next T-j turn R down to B6302 X-roads. SA up to New Brancepeth T-j

D ⬅ **two pages** **Either** turn L, then after 270 m (yd) 1st R 'Langley Moor' through Alum Waters to Langley Farm – reverse A to Star, **or** turn L down to railway path, then turn R along it to return to the start

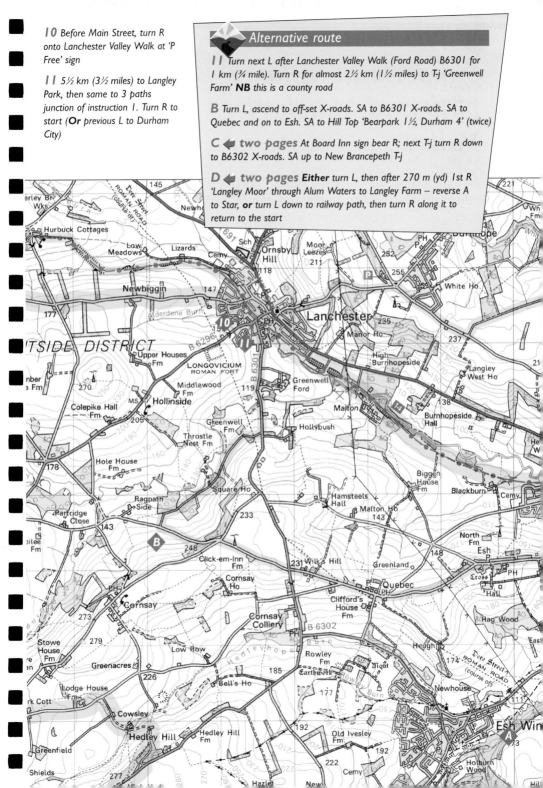

2 The Consett and Sunderland railway path and Lanchester Valley

Start

Beamish Country Park (GR 217537)

P As above

Distance and grade

42 km (26 miles) – short route 29 km (18 miles)

✎ Easy

Terrain

Railway paths nearly always follow valleys with, at worst, a gentle gradient; the land between valleys is always higher and this is where the hills are on this ride. The steep hill down into Lanchester needs care. Highest point – Consett 265 m (869 ft). Lowest point – Pelton Fell 70 m (230 ft)

Nearest railway

Chester-le-Street, 3 km (2 miles) east of the route

An interesting, combination route, which utilises an on-road link to connect two excellent railway paths; this circuit can be joined at any point thus avoiding the need to use a vehicle. Commencing at Beamish for descriptive purposes, a clockwise direction is chosen to take advantage of the steep downhill into the Lanchester Valley after first crossing the undulations north and west of Sacriston. The Lanchester Valley railway path is followed through rural County Durham to Lydgetts Lane junction to join Sustrans' Consett and Sunderland railway path and Coast to Coast route. The ex-steelworks town of Consett and its satellite communities is negotiated and a high-level track leads into Annfield Plain. Passing easily through the built up section, the open views and rural atmosphere return as the circuit is completed.

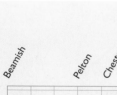

Beamish 1

The biggest open-air museum in Europe featuring all things historical of North East heritage; the Town, Colliery village, Railway Station, Home Farm and Pockerley Manor, all with every aspect of a Victorian community in living reality and accessible by tram, bus or on foot

Consett and Sunderland Railway Path

Owned by the 'paths for people' charity Sustrans (sustainable transport) and developed in conjunction with local Authorities; available for cyclists, walkers, wheelchairs and, where appropriate, horse riders. Look out for the spectacular Howns Gill Viaduct, built by Sir Thomas Bouch in 1857, which uses more than 2.5 million bricks. The C2C route shares a section of the railway path and is part of a much larger National Cycle Network. Straddling the North Pennines between the Irish Sea and the North Sea, the 224-km (140-mile) route follows minor roads and traffic-free cycle paths and won the Global Award for Green Tourism in 1996

▼ *Drift Mine, Beamish Museum*

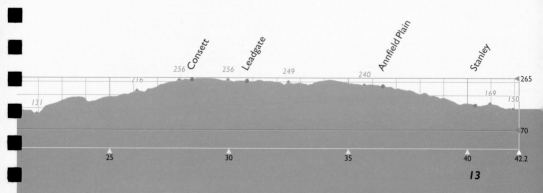

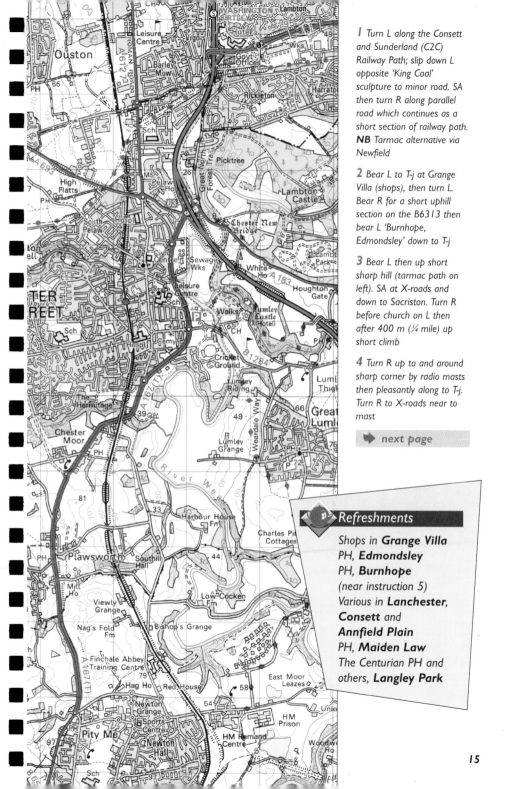

1 Turn L along the Consett and Sunderland (C2C) Railway Path; slip down L opposite 'King Coal' sculpture to minor road. SA then turn R along parallel road which continues as a short section of railway path. **NB** Tarmac alternative via Newfield

2 Bear L to T-j at Grange Villa (shops), then turn L. Bear R for a short uphill section on the B6313 then bear L 'Burnhope, Edmondsley' down to T-j

3 Bear L then up short sharp hill (tarmac path on left). SA at X-roads and down to Sacriston. Turn R before church on L then after 400 m (¼ mile) up short climb

4 Turn R up to and around sharp corner by radio masts then pleasantly along to T-j. Turn R to X-roads near to mast

➡ next page

◆ Refreshments

Shops in **Grange Villa**
PH, **Edmondsley**
PH, **Burnhope**
(near instruction 5)
Various in **Lanchester,
Consett** and
Annfield Plain
PH, **Maiden Law**
The Centurian PH and
others, **Langley Park**

5 *Take care*. Turn L, down steeply, to Lanchester. Cross A691 then SA for 220 m (yd) to Lanchester Valley Walk

Short cut

SA to Maiden Law X-roads (PH) then again SA and turn R 'Greencroft Industrial Estate' to rejoin railway path by small lake on left (see instruction 10)

6 Turn R and follow railway path through attractive countryside to Lydgett's Lane junction. Turn L for 400 m (½ mile) to the Howns Gill Viaduct then retrace

7 Turn R from Lanchester (SA from viaduct) and follow C2C directions (either stencils or small blue signs)

8 At Templetown turn L then turn R at

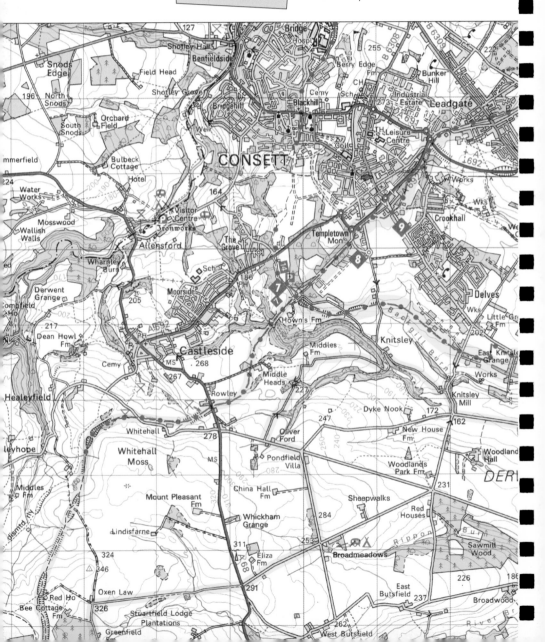

roundabout on marked cycle path. Cross road then after 220 m (yd) bear R to cross Delves Lane by Rover Garage (**take care**)

9 SA, then keep sports field on your right to roundabout. Cross by the marked cycle path, then SA to next roundabout (PH). Cross to diagonally opposite point, through the cycle maze and on past 'The

Transformers' sculpture to small lake (at instruction 10)

10 SA (see Short cut) opposite lake, then – **easy to miss** – cross A693 by new bridge. Through Annfield Plain, then follow Consett and Sunderland Railway Path to the start

◀ **two pages**

3 *Along the Tyne Valley from Haltwhistle*

Start

Haltwhistle Railway Station

P As above

Distance and grade

69 km (43 miles)

Easy/moderate

Terrain

Quiet roads and lanes through ever-changing scenery; some hills in the western half of the route but otherwise level. Highest point – Crindledykes corner 262 m (860 ft). Lowest point – Tyne Riverside Country Park 1m (3 ft)

Nearest railway

Haltwhistle

This ride is a linear route and follows the line of the picturesque Tyne Valley. From Haltwhistle, the usually quiet road to Bardon Mill is taken, then, leaving the valley floor behind, the cycle-friendly ascent into Hadrian's Wall country ensues. There is a short, rough section between the main entrance to Vindolanda and the museum at Chesterholm, after which the Roman road Stanegate leads eastwards to descend into Newbrough and on through Fourstones. A pleasant, scenic detour provides good views of the River North Tyne to rejoin the attractive riverside route into Hexham. There is some height gain beyond Hexham where the route splits to include Corbridge or to take in two castles before descending to the riverside for the remaining part of the ride; first Bywell then Ovingham followed by Low Prudhoe and Wylam until finally Newburn is reached – a most enjoyable expedition.

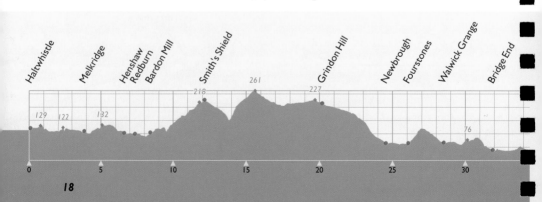

Vindolanda 3

Extensive site of Roman fort and settlement situated behind Hadrian's Wall with fine museum and reconstruction fort. Almost totally self-sufficient in all essentials, the fort was home for the occupying army from AD 80 for several centuries at different levels; it is still under permanent exploration; some 12000 artifacts are found each year and this is projected to continue for the next 150 years

Hexham 7

Since AD 674, Hexham's history has spanned the centuries: Hexham Abbey has 7th century origins; the Moot Hall was built in about 1400; a tall pillar of red sandstone marks the site of the old market now the centre of the Tuesday market next to the Shambles (long-roofed shelter) built in 1766; Tyne Bridge, built in 1793, is the first bridge over the river after the 'Meeting of the Waters' east of Warden

Halton Castle and Aydon Castle 9

Fine 14th-century fortified house chiefly composed of Roman stones; dignified little church largely rebuilt in 1706 again using Roman stones; interesting dove-cote and pond with resident ducks. Aydon Castle, built in 1300, is also in a fine situation and open to the public

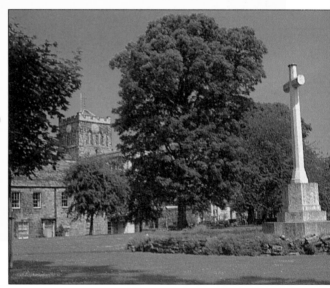

▶ Hexham Abbey and the memorial cross

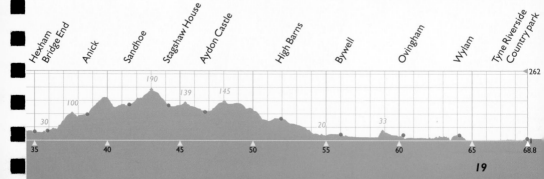

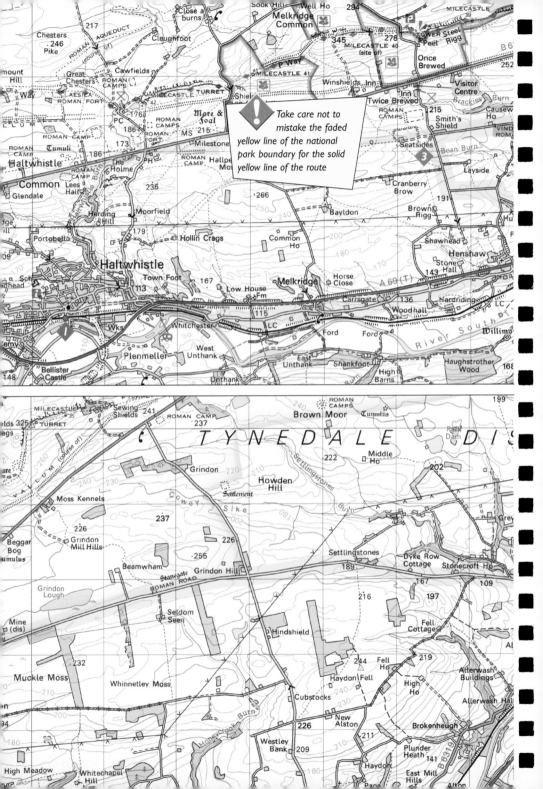

Take care not to mistake the faded yellow line of the national park boundary for the solid yellow line of the route

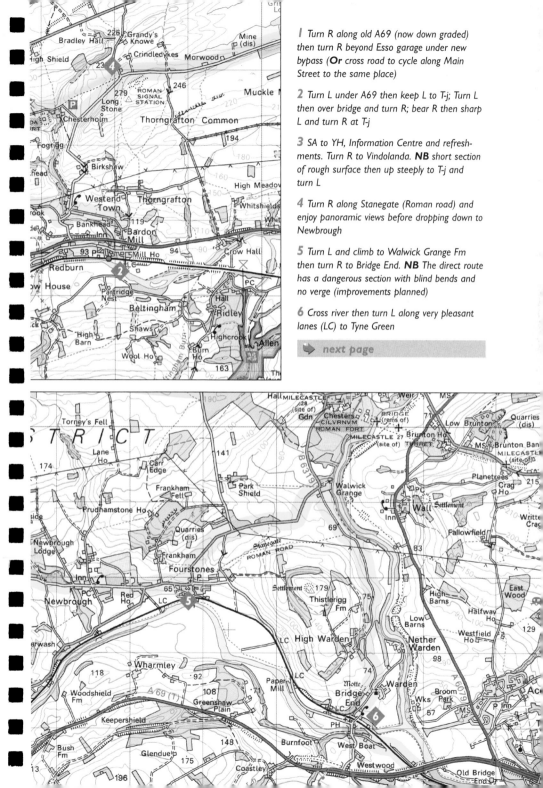

1 Turn R along old A69 (now down graded) then turn R beyond Esso garage under new bypass (**Or** cross road to cycle along Main Street to the same place)

2 Turn L under A69 then keep L to T-j; Turn L then over bridge and turn R; bear R then sharp L and turn R at T-j

3 SA to YH, Information Centre and refreshments. Turn R to Vindolanda. **NB** short section of rough surface then up steeply to T-j and turn L

4 Turn R along Stanegate (Roman road) and enjoy panoramic views before dropping down to Newbrough

5 Turn L and climb to Walwick Grange Fm then turn R to Bridge End. **NB** The direct route has a dangerous section with blind bends and no verge (improvements planned)

6 Cross river then turn L along very pleasant lanes (LC) to Tyne Green

next page

7 Turn R to visit Hexham then retrace to continue. Turn L and cross LC (**take care**), then on to L turn across Tyne Bridge. Turn L (bridleway) before roundabout which goes on to cross A69. Turn R, then L to X-roads and turn R

8 SA, then again SA through Oakwood. Turn L up to T-j then turn R to fork and bear R. At T-j turn L to the hamlet of Sandhoe. Bear R then SA up to A68

Alternative route

Follow marked route to visit Corbridge

9 **Take care**. Turn R down to next turning L to Halton Castle (**Or** SA, then turn 1st R for a superb descent into Corbridge). Returning from Halton, turn L to Aydon Castle

10 Turn R, then L and then cut back R down to B6530.

Turn L, then turn next R (**take care**) to descend to the banks of the River Tyne

11 SA and bear L at Bywell Bridge (**Or** SA then turn R at next X-roads to visit Bywell)

➡ **two pages**

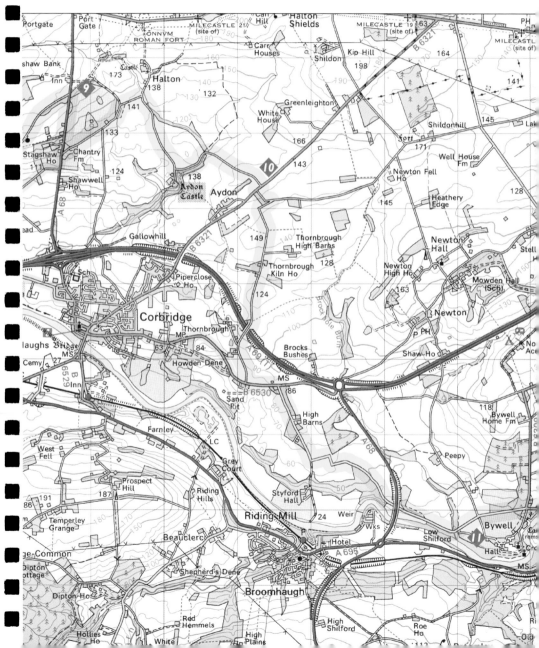

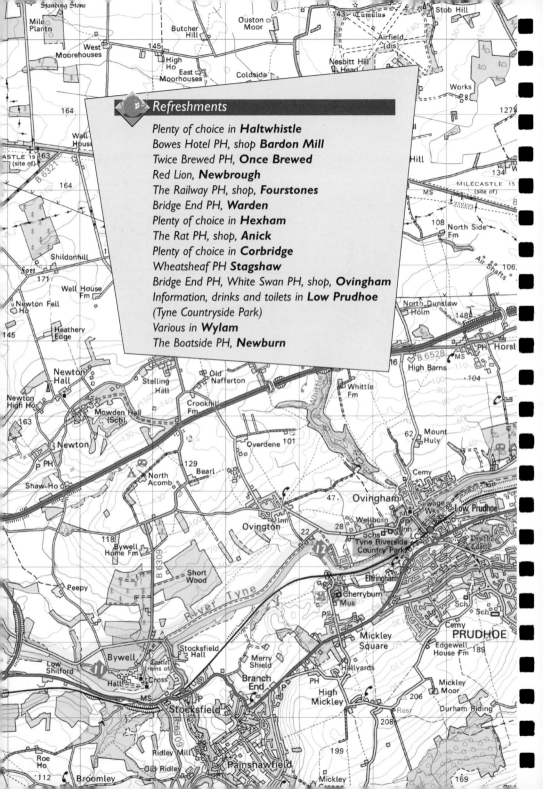

Refreshments

Plenty of choice in **Haltwhistle**

Bowes Hotel PH, shop **Bardon Mill**

Twice Brewed PH, **Once Brewed**

Red Lion, **Newbrough**

The Railway PH, shop, **Fourstones**

Bridge End PH, **Warden**

Plenty of choice in **Hexham**

The Rat PH, shop, **Anick**

Plenty of choice in **Corbridge**

Wheatsheaf PH **Stagshaw**

Bridge End PH, White Swan PH, shop, **Ovingham**

Information, drinks and toilets in **Low Prudhoe** (Tyne Countryside Park)

Various in **Wylam**

The Boatside PH, **Newburn**

12 *Bear R to Ovingham*
NB *superb packhorse bridge on R.
Turn R over metal bridge (***take
care***) then turn R into Tyne
Riverside Park (toilets). Pass under
bridge and follow riverside cycle
path past Hagg Fm*

13 *Turn L before the railway
bridge then cross West Wylam
Bridge; follow the railway path to
the road which leads to the
Country Park.*

NB *The route continues east to
Newcastle quayside and on to
North Shields (ferry terminals) and
Tynemouth. This is a Sustrans
Millenium Route and whilst most of
the route is in place, some new
sections and bridges will not be
completed until Easter 2000 but
on-road alternatives are possible*

4 From Stocksfield, to the north and south of the Tyne Valley

This route offers two excellent rides in one and, in the main, uses quiet lanes and minor roads. The Tyne Valley sections are flat and offer fine cycling through pleasant scenery and can be enjoyed at length (literally) in their own right. Stamfordham is a picturesque village surrounded by attractive countryside. The Cycle Route past Stephenson's Cottage is recommended for all bikes, as is the onward short-cut route across West Wylam Bridge to Prudhoe. The Southern loop requires more energy but not to any excessive degree, so do not be put off if you are reasonably fit. The uphill sections are amply rewarded with matching downhills and the refreshment points are well placed at suitable intervals.

Start
Stocksfield Railway Station

P As above

Distance and grade
62 km (39 miles) – short route 45 km (28 miles)

Moderate

Moderate/ strenuous with short cut

Terrain
Northern loop is pleasant and gentle. NB The Heddon-on-the-Wall descent is very steep! Southern loop is more challenging with some good views. Highest point – Greymare Hill 285 m (935 ft). Lowest point – the Tyne Valley

Nearest railway
Stocksfield

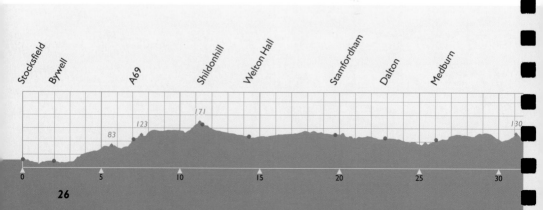

▼ *Prudhae Castle*

Bywell 2 *(short detour)*
Quiet site of historical interest but the original village has long gone; twin churches of St Andrews with its superb Saxon tower known as the White Church (Premontsratensian monks from nearby Blanchland) and St Peters, the Black from the black robed Benedictine monks of Durham. There is an ancient village cross, Bywell Castle (private) and 18th-century Bywell Hall – well worth further investigation

Wylam 10
Cottage birth-place of George Stephenson, the creator of railways, born in 1781; the arched West Wylam Bridge was an earlier construction design on which much larger and more famous bridges were modelled including The Tyne Bridge, The Wear Bridge at Sunderland and even the Sydney Harbour Bridge in Australia

The Lead Road 13/16
Until fairly recent times, lead ore was mined in the North Pennines and smelted at various locations. The lead was then taken by road to main ports or to be turned into pipes etc. at Blaydon on Tyne

Refreshments

Shop, **Stocksfield**
Bay Horse Inn, Swinburne Arms, **Stamfordham**
The Swan PH, Three Horse Shoes PH, **Heddon-on-the-Wall**
Tea room and others **Wylam**
Fox and Hounds PH, **Coalburns**
Three horse Shoes PH, **Leadgate**
Dr Syntax, **New Ridley**

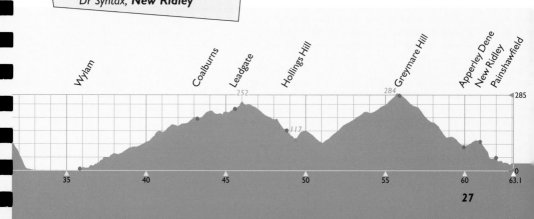

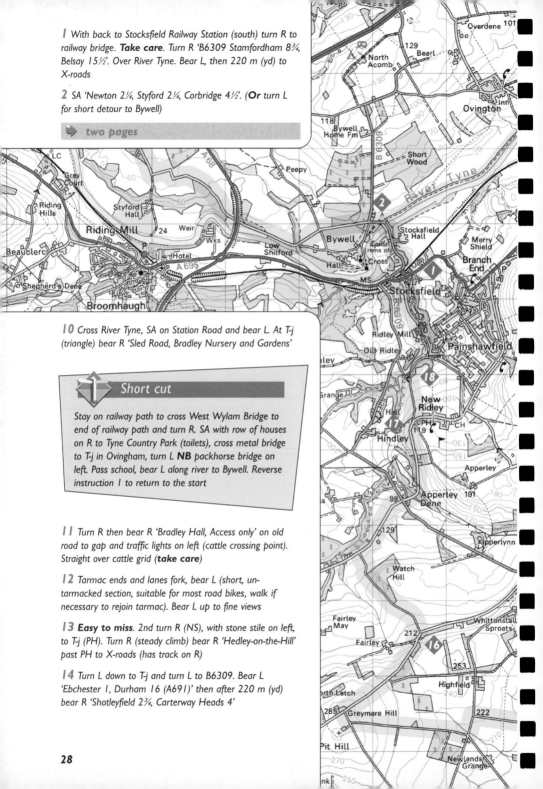

1 With back to Stocksfield Railway Station (south) turn R to railway bridge. **Take care**. Turn R 'B6309 Stamfordham 8¾, Belsay 15½'. Over River Tyne. Bear L, then 220 m (yd) to X-roads

2 SA 'Newton 2¼, Styford 2¼, Corbridge 4½'. (**Or** turn L for short detour to Bywell)

➡ **two pages**

10 Cross River Tyne, SA on Station Road and bear L. At T-j (triangle) bear R 'Sled Road, Bradley Nursery and Gardens'

Short cut

Stay on railway path to cross West Wylam Bridge to end of railway path and turn R. SA with row of houses on R to Tyne Country Park (toilets), cross metal bridge to T-j in Ovingham, turn L **NB** packhorse bridge on left. Pass school, bear L along river to Bywell. Reverse instruction I to return to the start

11 Turn R then bear R 'Bradley Hall, Access only' on old road to gap and traffic lights on left (cattle crossing point). Straight over cattle grid (**take care**)

12 Tarmac ends and lanes fork, bear L (short, un-tarmacked section, suitable for most road bikes, walk if necessary to rejoin tarmac). Bear L up to fine views

13 **Easy to miss**. 2nd turn R (NS), with stone stile on left, to T-j (PH). Turn R (steady climb) bear R 'Hedley-on-the-Hill' past PH to X-roads (has track on R)

14 Turn L down to T-j and turn L to B6309. Bear L 'Ebchester I, Durham 16 (A691)' then after 220 m (yd) bear R 'Shotleyfield 2¾, Carterway Heads 4'

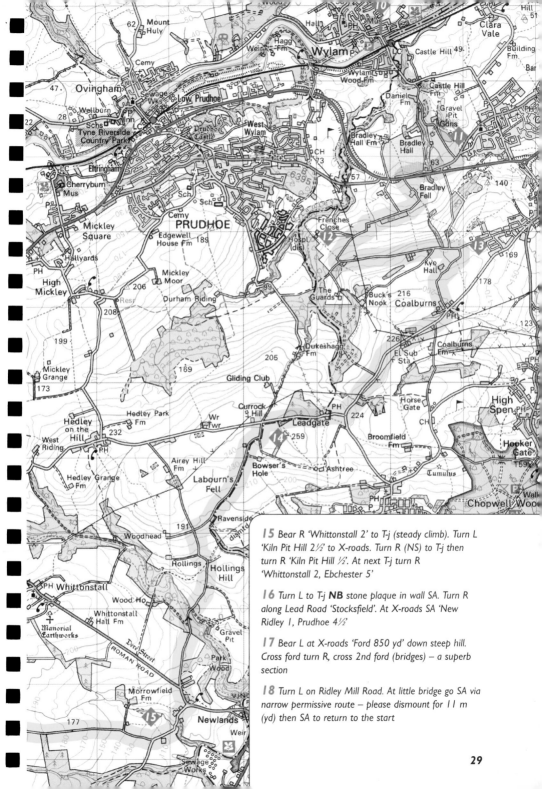

15 Bear R 'Whittonstall 2' to T-j (steady climb). Turn L 'Kiln Pit Hill 2½' to X-roads. Turn R (NS) to T-j then turn R 'Kiln Pit Hill ½'. At next T-j turn R 'Whittonstall 2, Ebchester 5'

16 Turn L to T-j **NB** stone plaque in wall SA. Turn R along Lead Road 'Stocksfield'. At X-roads SA 'New Ridley 1, Prudhoe 4½'

17 Bear L at X-roads 'Ford 850 yd' down steep hill. Cross ford turn R, cross 2nd ford (bridges) – a superb section

18 Turn L on Ridley Mill Road. At little bridge go SA via narrow permissive route – please dismount for 11 m (yd) then SA to return to the start

3 Turn L – **take care** – then after 400 m (¼ mile) turn R 'Thornbrough ½, Aydon 2' to fork, bear R (NS)

4 Bear R 'Welton 2, Stelling 2¼. X-roads SA 'Welton 1, Stelling 5'

5 SA 'Stamfordham 4'. SA at X-roads 'Stamfordham 3, Belsay 9'. Zigzag to Stamfordham!

6 SA 'Ponteland 6, Newcastle 13¾'

7 SA 'Dalton 1¼, Ponteland 5¼ over bridge bear R. T-j turn R 'Newburn 6, Wylam 8, Newcastle 10'

8 Turn R 'Stamfordham 5, Matfen 8½. **Easy to miss**. 270 m (yd) **after** next farm on R turn L 'Single Track Road, Unsuitable for HGVs'. Turn R (in effect SA)

9 For Wylam via railway path turn L before petrol station, then next R 'Heddon ¼. **NB** Hadrian's Wall on L. Turn L just after bus shelter (NS) 'Station Road leading to Heddon Haughs' after 27 m (yd). PH 110 m (yd) beyond bus shelter. Long stretch downhill through farm to railway path, turn R to Wylam (toilets)

Alternative route

Wylam by road. SA passing petrol station, then turn L 'Close House ½ to Wylam. Turn L 'Crawcrook 1½, Station ¼, RVI Castle Hill ¾' (PH, shops, toilets)

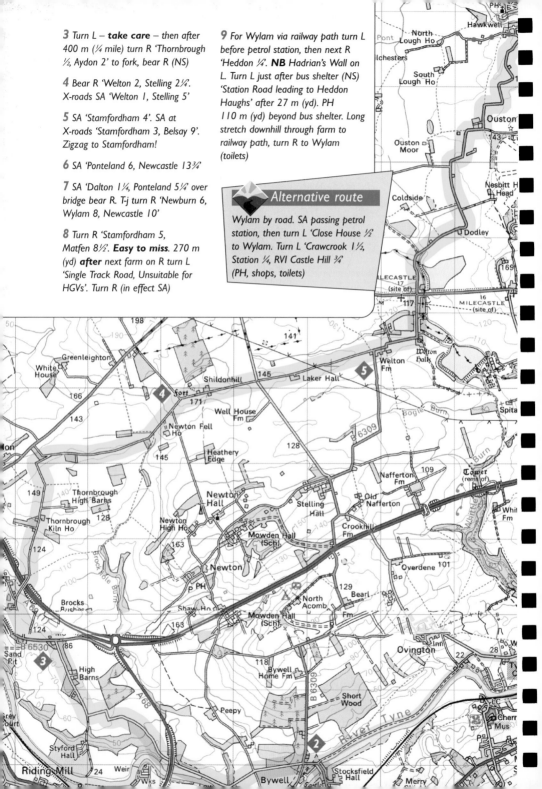

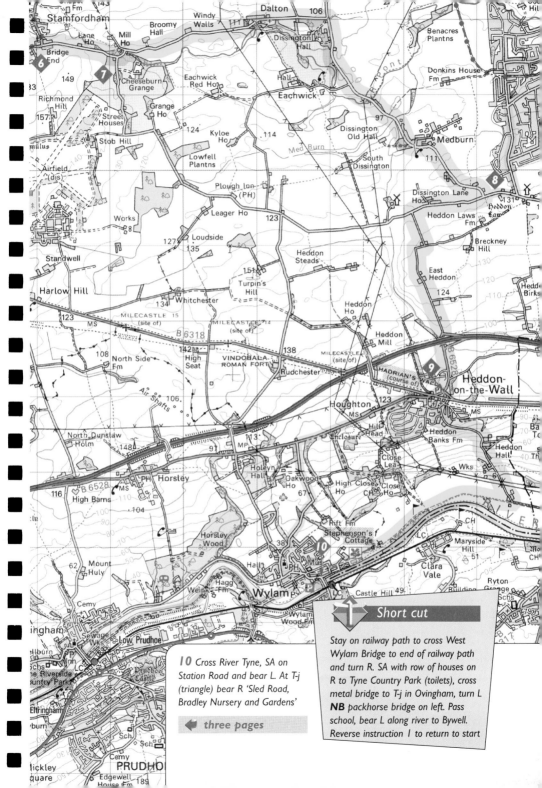

10 Cross River Tyne, SA on Station Road and bear L. At T-j (triangle) bear R 'Sled Road, Bradley Nursery and Gardens'

← *three pages*

↑→ **Short cut**

Stay on railway path to cross West Wylam Bridge to end of railway path and turn R. SA with row of houses on R to Tyne Country Park (toilets), cross metal bridge to T-j in Ovingham, turn L **NB** *packhorse bridge on left. Pass school, bear L along river to Bywell. Reverse instruction 1 to return to start*

The north Tyne Valley, east of Bellingham and west of Wark

As with any route, grading is always prone to subjectivity and that is without attempting to take into account the many variables such as weather, bike condition and fitness. This tour is graded Moderate/strenuous because if it is windy, it will tend to lean toward the category of Strenuous due to its position. This is a fine ride and would merit inclusion in any guide book, so pick your day and go for it. Following the River North Tyne to Gunnerton, the ride climbs gently and pleasantly northwards to offer magnificent views of the surrounding fells and distant Kielder Forest. The long, narrow downhill past Sweethope Lough leads on to East and West Woodburn before the scenic but steady climb, which precedes the steep descent into Bellingham. The route climbs out of the valley and on over rolling pasture land to circumnavigate the edge of Wark Forest whilst offering a superb array of ever-changing vistas before threading its way back to Wark.

Start

Village green, Wark

P 1 km (¾ mile) north of Wark on east side of river, opposite Gold Island

Distance and grade

62 km (39 miles) – short route 45 km (28 miles)

Moderate/strenuous

Terrain

Largely undulating, this hilly ride has marvellous views and can be ridden in either direction. Highest point – Green Rigg 291 m (955 ft). Lowest point – Wark 78 m (257 ft)

Nearest railway

Hexham, 13 km (8 miles) south of instruction 2

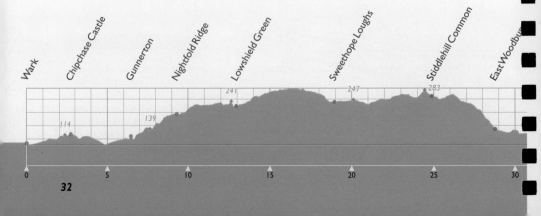

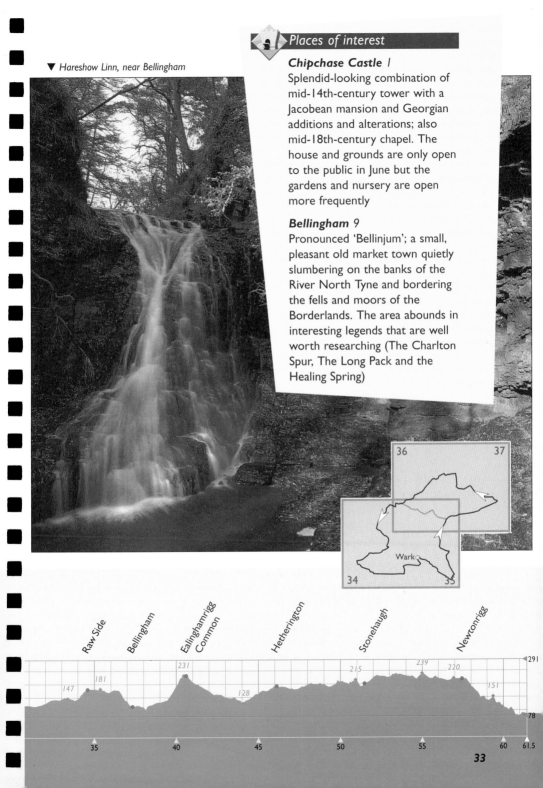

▼ Hareshow Linn, near Bellingham

Chipchase Castle 1

Splendid-looking combination of mid-14th-century tower with a Jacobean mansion and Georgian additions and alterations; also mid-18th-century chapel. The house and grounds are only open to the public in June but the gardens and nursery are open more frequently

Bellingham 9

Pronounced 'Bellinjum'; a small, pleasant old market town quietly slumbering on the banks of the River North Tyne and bordering the fells and moors of the Borderlands. The area abounds in interesting legends that are well worth researching (The Charlton Spur, The Long Pack and the Healing Spring)

36   37

Wark

34   35

Raw Side · Bellingham · Ealinghamrigg Common · Hetherington · Stonehaugh · Newtonrigg

147   181   231   128   215   239   220   151

291   78

35   40   45   50   55   60   61.5

33

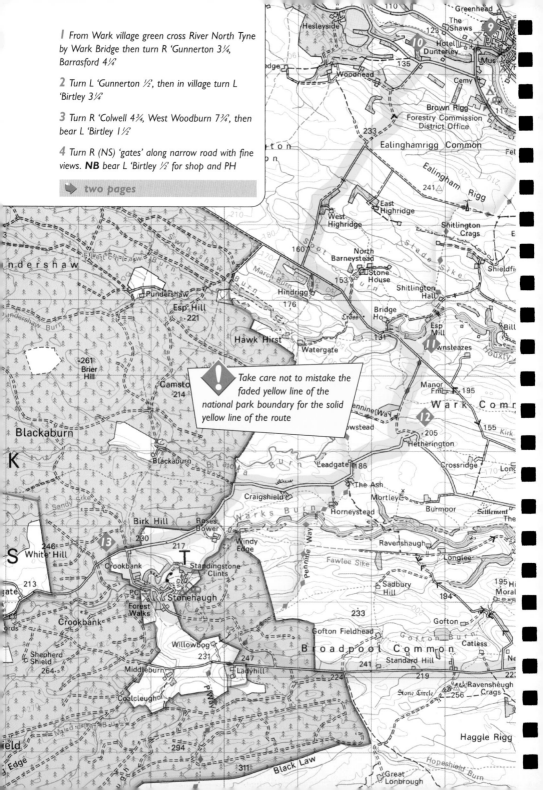

1 From Wark village green cross River North Tyne by Wark Bridge then turn R 'Gunnerton 3¼, Barrasford 4¼'

2 Turn L 'Gunnerton ½', then in village turn L 'Birtley 3¼'

3 Turn R 'Colwell 4¾, West Woodburn 7¾', then bear L 'Birtley 1½'

4 Turn R (NS) 'gates' along narrow road with fine views. **NB** bear L 'Birtley ½' for shop and PH

➡ two pages

! Take care not to mistake the faded yellow line of the national park boundary for the solid yellow line of the route

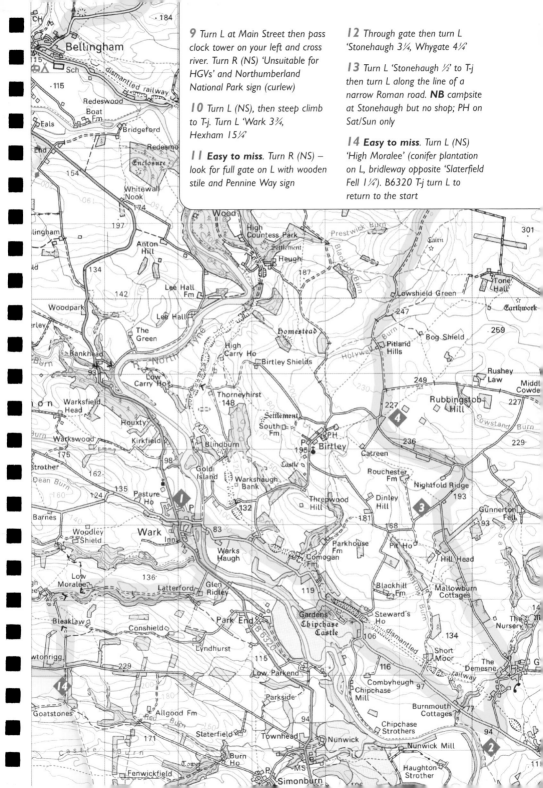

9 Turn L at Main Street then pass clock tower on your left and cross river. Turn R (NS) 'Unsuitable for HGVs' and Northumberland National Park sign (curlew)

10 Turn L (NS), then steep climb to T-j. Turn L 'Wark 3¾, Hexham 15¼'

11 Easy to miss. Turn R (NS) – look for full gate on L with wooden stile and Pennine Way sign

12 Through gate then turn L 'Stonehaugh 3¼, Whygate 4¼'

13 Turn L 'Stonehaugh ½' to T-j then turn L along the line of a narrow Roman road. **NB** campsite at Stonehaugh but no shop; PH on Sat/Sun only

14 Easy to miss. Turn L (NS) 'High Moralee' (conifer plantation on L, bridleway opposite 'Slaterfield Fell 1¼'). B6320 T-j turn L to return to the start

5 Turn R (NS) to A68 X-roads. SA on narrow road, pass Sweethope Loughs (lakes), then turn L on wider road 'West Woodburn 5'

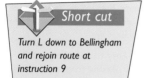

Short cut

Turn L down to Bellingham and rejoin route at instruction 9

6 Turn R for 380 m (yd) on A68 then turn R 'East Woodburn 1¼, Monkridge 4¼ – please **take care** and use the wide verge if necessary; do not wait in middle of road for R turn

7 Turn L (NS) to A68 then turn R – use footpath on R to access PH and shop and avoid crossing A68 twice

8 Turn L opposite PH 'Bellingham 4¼'

9 Turn L at Main Street then pass clock tower on your L and cross river. Turn R (NS) 'Unsuitable for HGVs' and Northumberland National Park sign (curlew)

◀ previous page

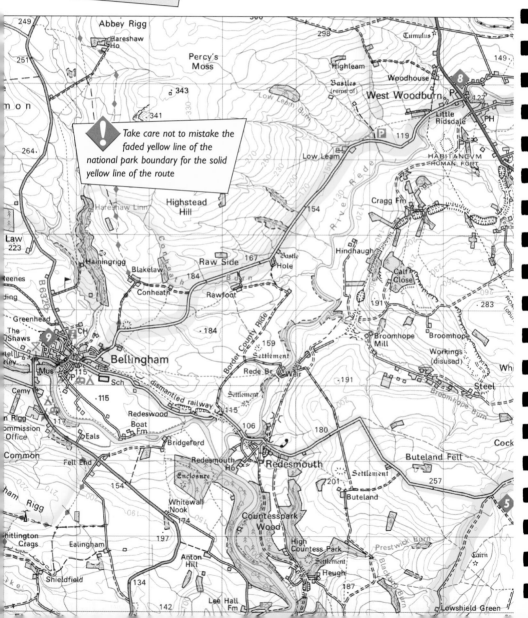

Take care not to mistake the faded yellow line of the national park boundary for the solid yellow line of the route

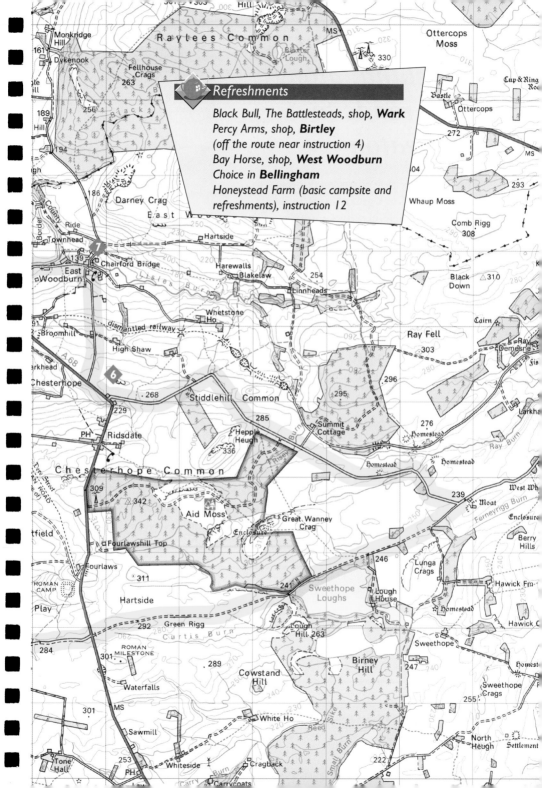

Refreshments

Black Bull, The Battlesteads, shop, **Wark**
Percy Arms, shop, **Birtley**
(off the route near instruction 4)
Bay Horse, shop, **West Woodburn**
Choice in **Bellingham**
Honeystead Farm (basic campsite and refreshments), instruction 12

6 *Northwest of Ponteland, along quiet roads to Capheaton*

Although this ride starts at Ponteland, Newcastle is not a great distance away. There is a choice of railway path or road through Darras Hall luxury estate to reach the Medburn road where the ride really begins. On to bonny Stamfordham with its spacious village green and old gaol house and then to the lovely village of Matfen. Northwards to Capheaton, noted for its attractive stone cottages – all of which give this ride a timeless feel. Narrow lanes run gently downhill through unspoilt country-side to end this truly enjoyable tour.

Start

Main Street or Darras Hall, Ponteland

P Parking behind Station Cottages, Ponteland

Distance and grade

56 km (35 miles)

Easy/moderate

Terrain

Very gently but almost imperceptibly rising to the top of the loop and returning with the aid of gravity. Highest point – Ingoe Moor 230 m (755 ft). Lowest point – Ponteland 57 m (188 ft)

Nearest railway

Metro Station at Newcastle airport (folding bikes only)

Refreshments

Plenty of choice in **Ponteland**
Tea rooms, **Capheaton**
Black Bull 🍺🍴, shop, **Matfen**
Bay Horse, Swinburne Arms, shop, **Stamfordham**
Plough Inn 🍺 at instruction 2

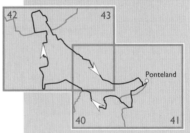

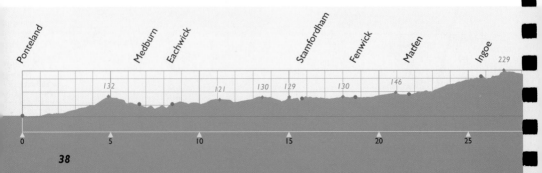

Belsay Hall, Castle and Gardens *(close to the route)* 10
Castle is 14th century, the Grecian style Hall is 19th century, 12 ha (30 acres) of landscaped gardens with a unique rock garden. Altogether a most remarkable country estate and well worth a visit

Capheaton Hall 9
Fine stone country house built in 1688 by Robert Trollope (also Netherwitton Hall) with matching estate cottages

Other Halls
Dissington Hall (unseen); Eachwick Hall (good view); Cheeseburn Grange near Stamfordham; Matfen Hall – a Cheshire Home recently converted into a golf club

▼ *Matfen Cross and houses*

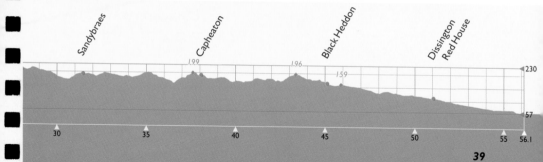

1 Pass Station Cottages to main road. Turn L, then next R at Nat West Bank. Pass War Memorial, then turn next R 'Runnymede Road' for 2½ km (1½ miles). Turn L for further 2½ km (1½ miles) to T-j. Turn R, then next R

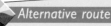

Alternative route

For Cycle Path through Darras Hall turn R at Nat West Bank, then turn L into park to bridge. Bear R then follow interesting cycle path. **Easy to miss**. At church cross road and cut behind shops then sharp R. At end of road **either** turn L to join main route, on to T-j, turn R then next R, **or**, for robust bikes, turn R then next L along bridleway to road above Medburn, then turn R

2 Turn L 'Eachwick ½, Wylam 5' to T-j then turn R 'Stamfordham 5, Matfen 8½'

3 Turn L 'Stamfordham 1, Matfen 4½' then turn R into Stamfordham. Bear L at large grass triangle **NB** old gaol on the right

➡ next page

10 Join B6309 (in effect SA) then next R. Turn R for more gentle downhill along quiet narrow lanes

11 Turn L (**Or** SA to reverse the alternatvie route to return to the start)

12 Turn R (busy road – but there is a footpath as far as the bend). Turn R after bend down Fox Covert Lane then next L to reverse instruction 1 back to the start

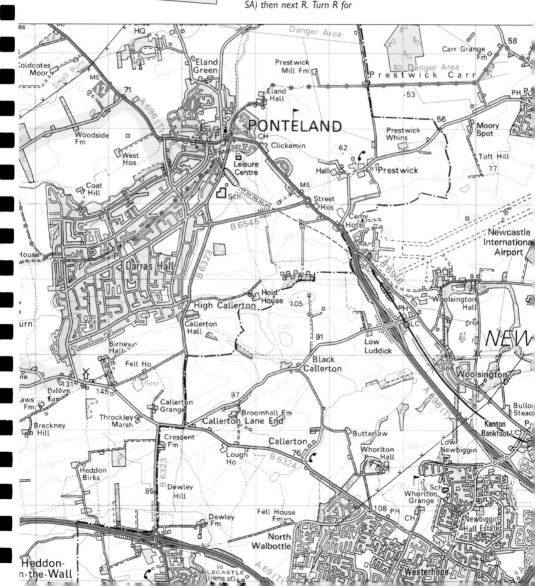

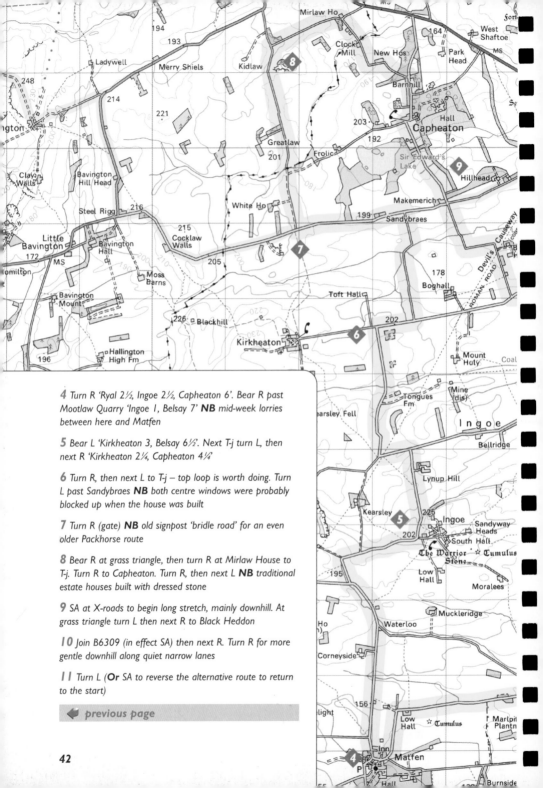

4 Turn R 'Ryal 2½, Ingoe 2½, Capheaton 6'. Bear R past Mootlaw Quarry 'Ingoe 1, Belsay 7' **NB** mid-week lorries between here and Matfen

5 Bear L 'Kirkheaton 3, Belsay 6½'. Next T-j turn L, then next R 'Kirkheaton 2¼, Capheaton 4¼'

6 Turn R, then next L to T-j – top loop is worth doing. Turn L past Sandybraes **NB** both centre windows were probably blocked up when the house was built

7 Turn R (gate) **NB** old signpost 'bridle road' for an even older Packhorse route

8 Bear R at grass triangle, then turn R at Mirlaw House to T-j. Turn R to Capheaton. Turn R, then next L **NB** traditional estate houses built with dressed stone

9 SA at X-roads to begin long stretch, mainly downhill. At grass triangle turn L then next R to Black Heddon

10 Join B6309 (in effect SA) then next R. Turn R for more gentle downhill along quiet narrow lanes

11 Turn L (**Or** SA to reverse the alternative route to return to the start)

◀ previous page

Westward to Wallington from Morpeth of Mitford

The countryside that lies to the west of Morpeth is nothing short of a rural treasure trove in terms of cottages and mansions, rivers and ravines, woods and farmsteads, lakes, castles and crags. The scenery is as varied as the ride itself – changing character dramatically as the route unfolds. At first, the roads are wide and full of purpose but gradually they change to reveal hidden gems by the side of the picturesque ribbons along which you ride. Whilst numerous large houses are visible in this area, Wallington Hall is the centre-piece and this stately home can be easily seen from the road as you cycle past. The busy A696 is crossed twice at right angles and the route passes close to the Great and Little Wanney. These are two north-facing crags extruding from the windswept fells, which this route ventures across using unbeliev-ably quiet and narrow byways. Bolam Lake Country Park is visited on the return leg but this journey of discovery saves the best till last.

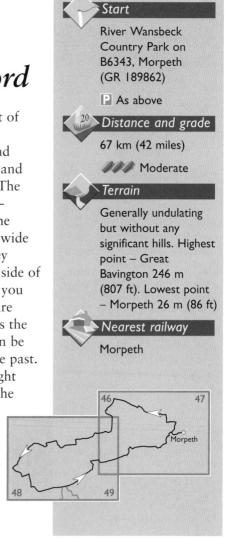

Start

River Wansbeck Country Park on B6343, Morpeth (GR 189862)

P As above

Distance and grade

67 km (42 miles)

Moderate

Terrain

Generally undulating but without any significant hills. Highest point – Great Bavington 246 m (807 ft). Lowest point – Morpeth 26 m (86 ft)

Nearest railway

Morpeth

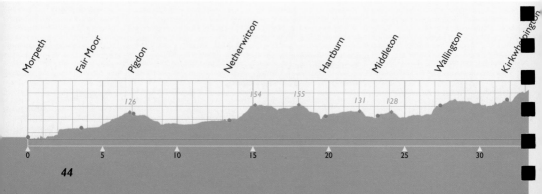

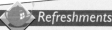
Plenty of choice in
Morpeth
Plough Inn, **Mitford**
The Ox Inn,
Middleton
The Stable Coffee
Shop, **Bolam West
Houses**
(near instruction 14)
Dyke Neuk 🥾🥾,
off the route north
of **Meldon**

Places of interest

Morpeth 1
An ancient and attractive town that lies
on a peninsula of the River Wansbeck.
Morpeth is said to be the most beautiful town in the county. Numerous interesting buildings and architectural styles;
Museum of Northumbrian bagpipes

Wallington Hall 6
Built by Sir William Blackett near the
middle of 18th century, later owned by
the Trevelyan family who eventually gave
it and its large estate to become one of
the first National Trust properties. Has
French Chateau style and is full of artis-
tic interest – a very worthwhile visit

▼ The Clock Tower, Wallington Hall

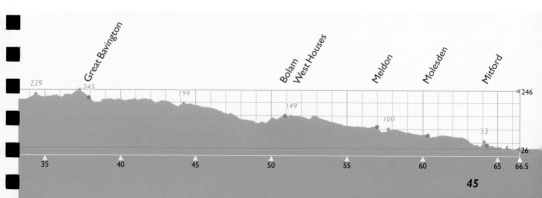

1 West along the B6343 to Mitford. Turn R before bridge **NB** old sign 'St Leonard's Road, Benridge, Pigdon', up short, steep hill to T-j

2 Turn L 'Netherwitton 6½, Pigdon 2½, Stanton 4¾'. Keep R at bend, turn L 'Pigdon 1, Netherwitton 4'. L then R near Stanton

3 Over bridge then turn L 'Longwitton, Cambo'. Follow Z bend, then turn L 'Meldon 4, Morpeth 8'

4 Turn R 'Hartburn 1¾, Scot's Gap 5'. Turn R (NS) at T-j on B6343 to Hartburn cross

15 Turn L 'Whalton 4, Bolam ¾' **NB** Bolam Hall has reverse 'ha ha' (sunken field behind wall on L, to retain stock without wall being visible)

16 Bear L (NS) over old railway bridge, then bear L 'Meldon Village'. Turn R 'Molesden 1¾' bear R at 'No Entry'. **NB** Pill box on L – this road was defended in World War 2! Bear L at West Coldside 'No Entry' to Mitford

17 At T-j turn R, then next R after weir. Turn L after 650 m (yd) to town centre

4 Turn R 'Hartburn 1¾, Scot's Gap 5'. Turn R (NS) at T-j on B6343 to Hartburn cross

5 Bear L 'Angerton 1, Middleton 2' SA 'Middleton 1¾' **NB** old bridge in field past PH. Turn L at T-j 'Bolam 3½, Belsay 5, Cambo 2½'

6 At T-j turn R. At ornate bridge T-j turn R to pass Wallington Hall

7 At X-roads turn L 'Kirkwhelpington'. Turn L at public telephone 'toilets', then bear R to A696

8 **Take care**. SA 'Carrycoates 6, Great Bavington 4, Plashetts 2½'

9 Turn L 'Great Bavington 1' **NB** Whinsill Fault, columnar dolerite rock's reappearance between Roman Wall and Craster

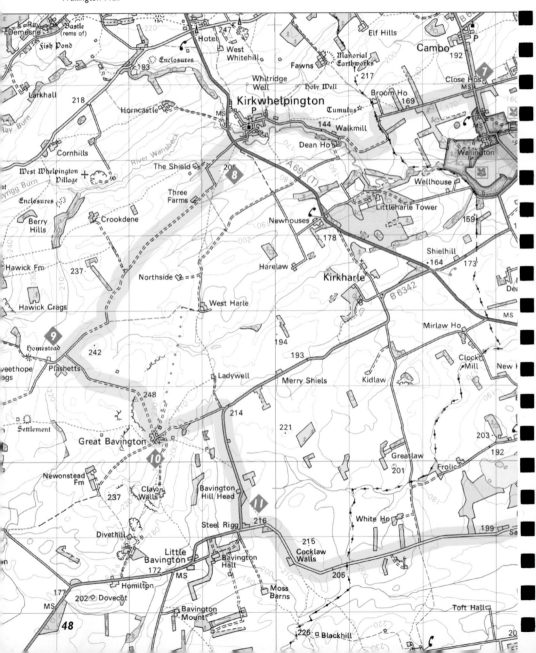

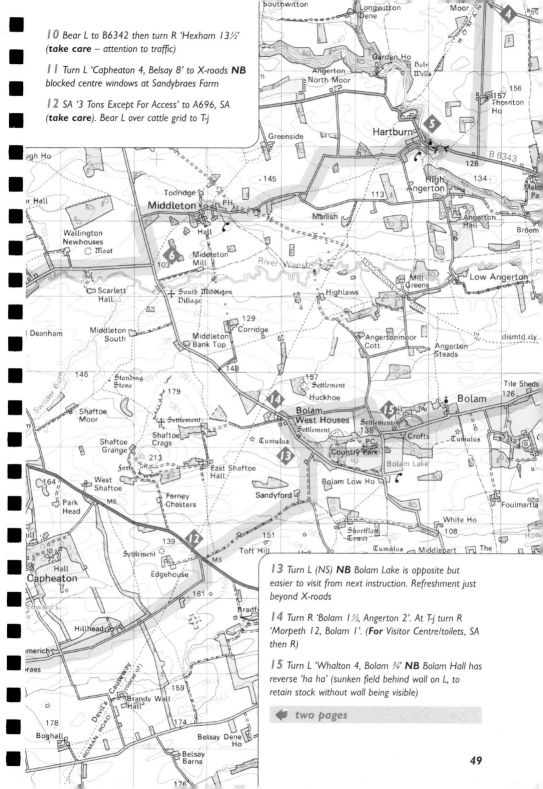

10 Bear L to B6342 then turn R 'Hexham 13½' (**take care** – attention to traffic)

11 Turn L 'Capheaton 4, Belsay 8' to X-roads **NB** blocked centre windows at Sandybraes Farm

12 SA '3 Tons Except For Access' to A696, SA (**take care**). Bear L over cattle grid to T-j

13 Turn L (NS) **NB** Bolam Lake is opposite but easier to visit from next instruction. Refreshment just beyond X-roads

14 Turn R 'Bolam 1½, Angerton 2'. At T-j turn R 'Morpeth 12, Bolam 1'. (**For** Visitor Centre/toilets, SA then R)

15 Turn L 'Whalton 4, Bolam ¾' **NB** Bolam Hall has reverse 'ha ha' (sunken field behind wall on L, to retain stock without wall being visible)

◄ two pages

Northeast of Morpeth to Cresswell on the coast

Morpeth is an ideal starting point. This is a short ride as it fits into the neat rectangle that has the A1 and the A1068 on the vertical sides and the A197 and B6345 on the horizontals. It is, nevertheless, a circular ride and crosses two of the main roads in relative safety to include the first of a series of visits to the magnificent Northumbrian coastline. Out of Morpeth, via pretty Bothal, the urban fringe is gradually left behind as you progress easily and pleasantly towards the coast. The route heads northwards with dunes on your right hand and the taste of the salt air on your lips before cutting inland past Widdrington. Quiet country roads lead on through Tritlington and Hebron until you emerge on the outskirts of Morpeth. There are two large opencast workings, which are located in the centre of this ride, but be assured, they are well screened and should not spoil your enjoyment.

Start

Morpeth Railway Station

P As above, free car park

Distance and grade

43 km (27 miles) – short route 26 km (16 miles)

Easy

Terrain

Almost completely flat apart from two short, sharp hills at Bothal Bank and Fulbeck Bank. Highest point – Earsdon 114 m (374 ft). Lowest point – near Druridge 1 m (3 ft)

Nearest railway

Morpeth

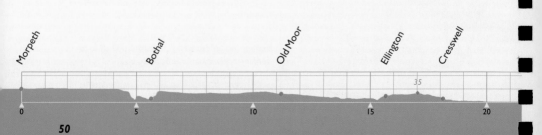

▶ *The River Wansbeck and St. George's Church, Morpeth*

Places of interest

Bothal 2

Picturesque hamlet close to the wooded River Wansbeck; substantial stone cottages guarded over by the remains of the ancient 13th-century castle built by Robert Bartram as a smaller scale Dunstanburgh Castle. View of tall, stately gatehouse and nearby is the fine 13th-century church with 14th-century alterations and additions

Cresswell and Widdrington 6/7

Old fishing village with 14th-century Cresswell tower house or peel tower where unspoilt sandy beaches turn to rugged cliffs. Fresh-water Nature Reserve at Druridge Links; Chibburn Presbytery, a 14th-century house of the Knights of St John of Jerusalem recently restored. Druridge Bay has nature reserves and several kilometres of dunes and wide sandy beaches. Widdrington was the location of a little-known French landing in 1692

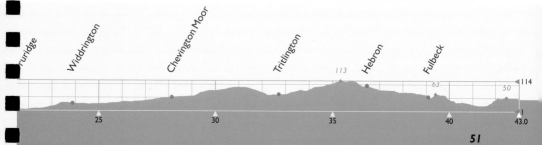

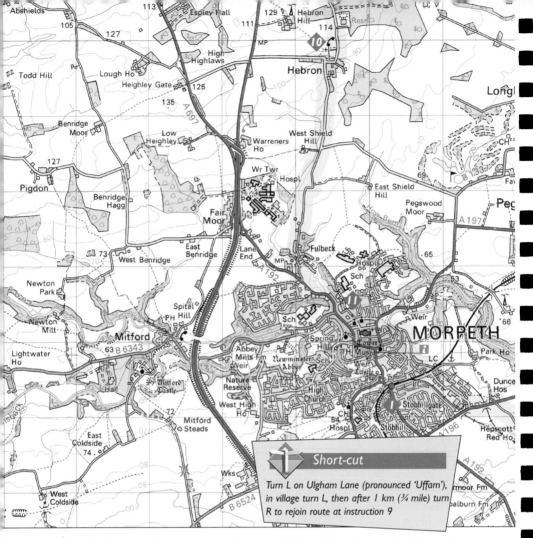

Short-cut

Turn L on Ulgham Lane (pronounced 'Uffam'), in village turn L, then after 1 km (¾ mile) turn R to rejoin route at instruction 9

1 Set off with the main line on your L over LC (sidings). After railway footbridge turn R through small industrial estate to A196. Turn L over bridge (path) then turn R (NS). At T-j turn L (NS)

2 Turn R then L (almost SA) 'Bothal 1¼, Pegswood 1½' to A1068

3 Cross over to path opposite then keep R of A197 for 165 m (yd) to cyclists crossing point (islands). Turn L back along cycle path (north side of A197) to T-j, then turn R 'Longhirst'

4 Keep R to T-j beyond LC. SA to A1068 and turn L, on to obvious T-j at instruction 5

5 Turn L 'Linton ½', then after 220 m (yd) bear R along rail path to cross A1068 to T-j

two pages

10 Turn L 'Morpeth, Longhirst, Pegswood' then, after just over 1 km (¾ mile), bear R (in effect SA) at grass triangle. At A192 turn L to traffic lights

11 Turn L 'Manchester Street', then turn R, then L to A197 T-j. Turn R to mini roundabout, then turn L keeping 'Old Red Bull PH' on your L. **Easy to miss** turn R, then L by Ambulance Station to cross River Wansbeck (bridge). Up to LC (mainline) to return to start

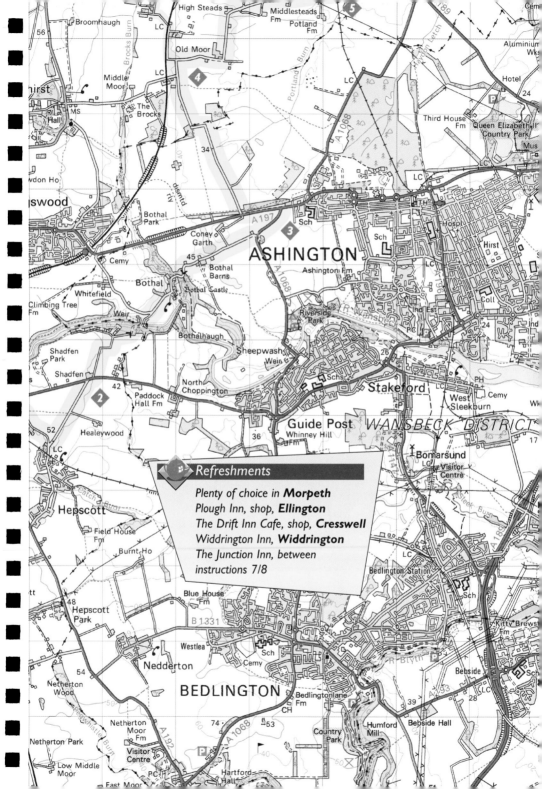

Refreshments

Plenty of choice in **Morpeth**
Plough Inn, shop, **Ellington**
The Drift Inn Cafe, shop, **Cresswell**
Widdrington Inn, **Widdrington**
The Junction Inn, between
instructions 7/8

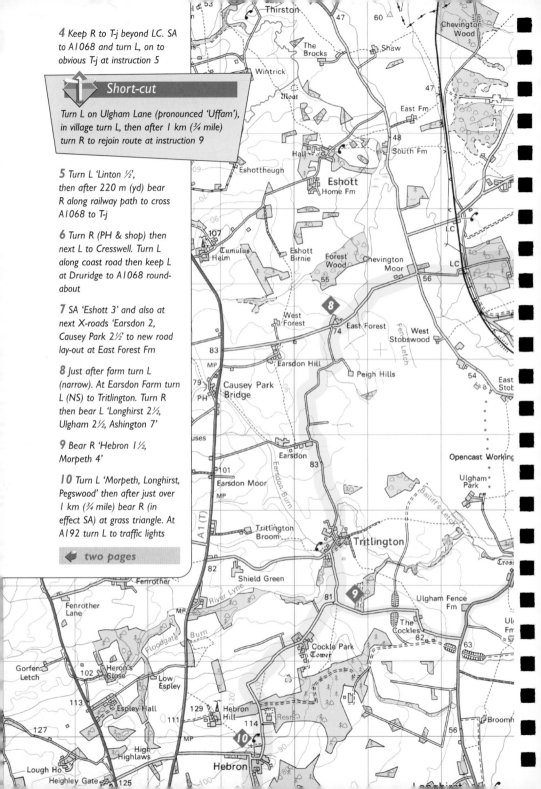

4 Keep R to T-j beyond LC. SA to A1068 and turn L, on to obvious T-j at instruction 5

⬆ Short-cut

Turn L on Ulgham Lane (pronounced 'Uffam'), in village turn L, then after 1 km (¾ mile) turn R to rejoin route at instruction 9

5 Turn L 'Linton ½', then after 220 m (yd) bear R along railway path to cross A1068 to T-j

6 Turn R (PH & shop) then next L to Cresswell. Turn L along coast road then keep L at Druridge to A1068 round-about

7 SA 'Eshott 3' and also at next X-roads 'Earsdon 2, Causey Park 2½' to new road lay-out at East Forest Fm

8 Just after farm turn L (narrow). At Earsdon Farm turn L (NS) to Tritlington. Turn R then bear L 'Longhirst 2½, Ulgham 2½, Ashington 7'

9 Bear R 'Hebron 1½, Morpeth 4'

10 Turn L 'Morpeth, Longhirst, Pegswood' then after just over 1 km (¾ mile) bear R (in effect SA) at grass triangle. At A192 turn L to traffic lights

◀ **two pages**

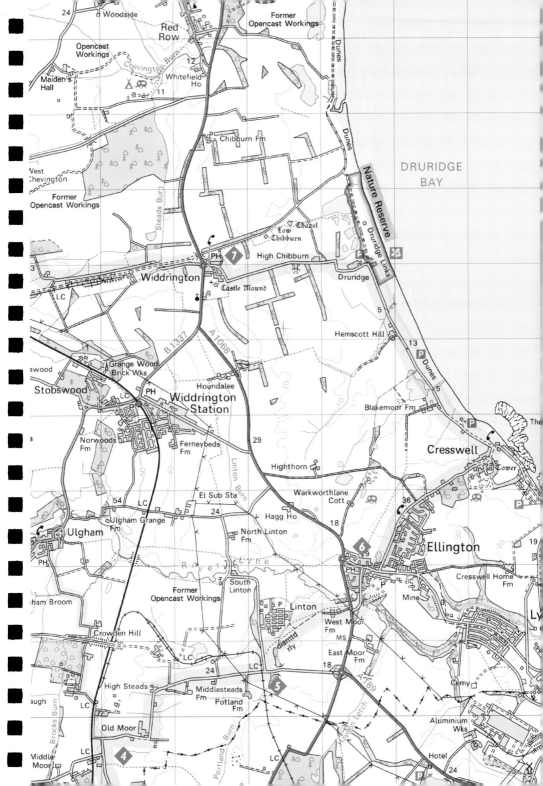

9 *Northwest of Morpeth to Rothbury, returning via The Fords*

Northumberland is full of gems and Rothbury is one of them. Being in a valley, hills are inevitable but this tour uses the contours to the best advantage, hence the ride's figure-of-eight shape. The final loop takes the line of least resistance to first of all drop into the utterly charming Coquet Valley and then to climb back out again for the return journey. There is an optional loop at the start of the tour and numerous short-cut possibilities in between. The full circuit to Rothbury via the descent to Great Tosson is recommended for the exceptional views of the Cheviot Hills and the surrounding countryside, which this section of the route affords. The cycling prior to this point and throughout the return route is no less enjoyable and the three fords are as picturesque as they are unexpected.

Start

River Wansbeck Country Park on B6343, Morpeth (GR 189862)

P As above

Distance and grade

69 km (43 miles) – short route 50 km (31 miles)

🚵🚵🚵🚵 Moderate/strenuous

Terrain

Predominantly quiet rural roads; a wonderful circuit with many options – can be done either way. The three fords are located at the bottom of short sharp descents/ascents and all need care. Highest point – Simonsides 247 m (810 ft). Lowest point – Morpeth 26 m (86 ft)

Nearest railway

Morpeth

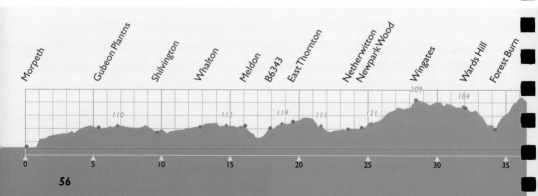

Meldon 3 *and* Netherwitton 5

Disused Morpeth/Rothbury railway line which remains almost fully intact but in multiownership. A small and humble 13th-century church with tomb of Sir William Fenwick in full armour – the bridge over the Wansbeck is said to be haunted by his wife 'Meg o Meldon'. Attractive double-arched bridge (near instruction 5) beyond which lies the 17th-century Netherwitton Hall built by Anthony Trollope; Newpark Wood is noted for the King and Queen oaks

Rothbury 9

The capital of Coquetdale surrounded by fascinating history and misty legends; Lordenshaw is a large, prehistoric camp containing many 'cup and ring' marked rocks whose meaning is not understood. Newton Park is part of the great deer park enclosed by Robert Rogerson in 1275; the road follows an ancient packhorse route to Great Tosson with its 10 m (33 ft) high peel tower

▲ *Coquet Valley, near Rohbury*

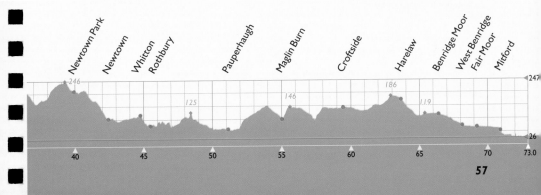

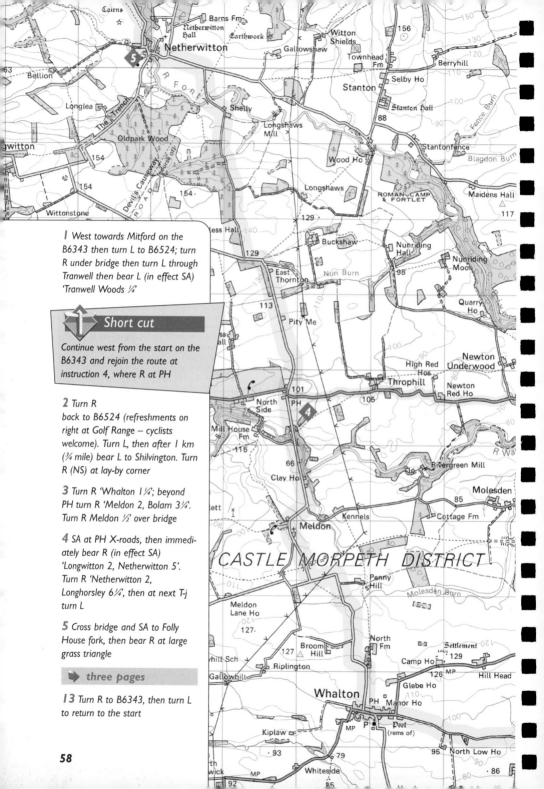

1 West towards Mitford on the B6343 then turn L to B6524; turn R under bridge then turn L through Tranwell then bear L (in effect SA) 'Tranwell Woods ¼'

Short cut

Continue west from the start on the B6343 and rejoin the route at instruction 4, where R at PH

2 Turn R
back to B6524 (refreshments on right at Golf Range – cyclists welcome). Turn L, then after 1 km (¾ mile) bear L to Shilvington. Turn R (NS) at lay-by corner

3 Turn R 'Whalton 1¼'; beyond PH turn R 'Meldon 2, Bolam 3¼'. Turn R Meldon ½' over bridge

4 SA at PH X-roads, then immediately bear R (in effect SA) 'Longwitton 2, Netherwitton 5'. Turn R 'Netherwitton 2, Longhorsley 6¼', then at next T-j turn L

5 Cross bridge and SA to Folly House fork, then bear R at large grass triangle

➡ **three pages**

13 Turn R to B6343, then turn L to return to the start

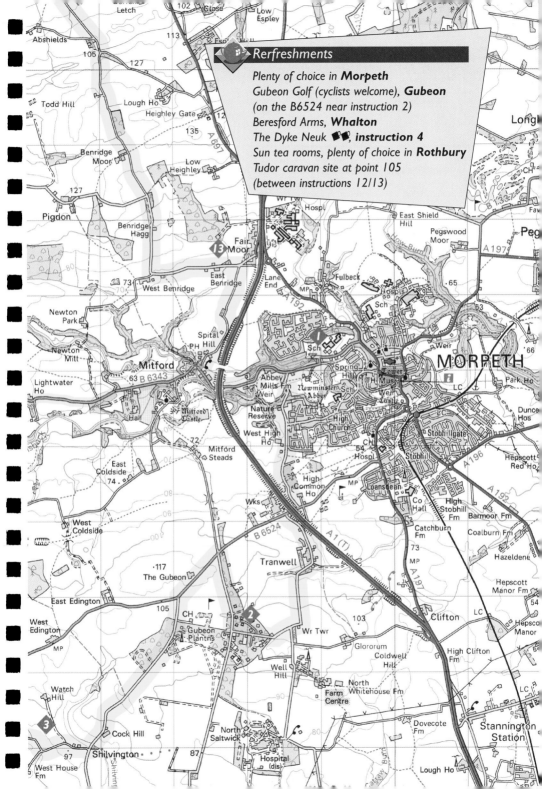

Rerfreshments

Plenty of choice in **Morpeth**
Gubeon Golf (cyclists welcome), **Gubeon**
(on the B6524 near instruction 2)
Beresford Arms, **Whalton**
The Dyke Neuk, **instruction** 4
Sun tea rooms, plenty of choice in **Rothbury**
Tudor caravan site at point 105
(between instructions 12/13)

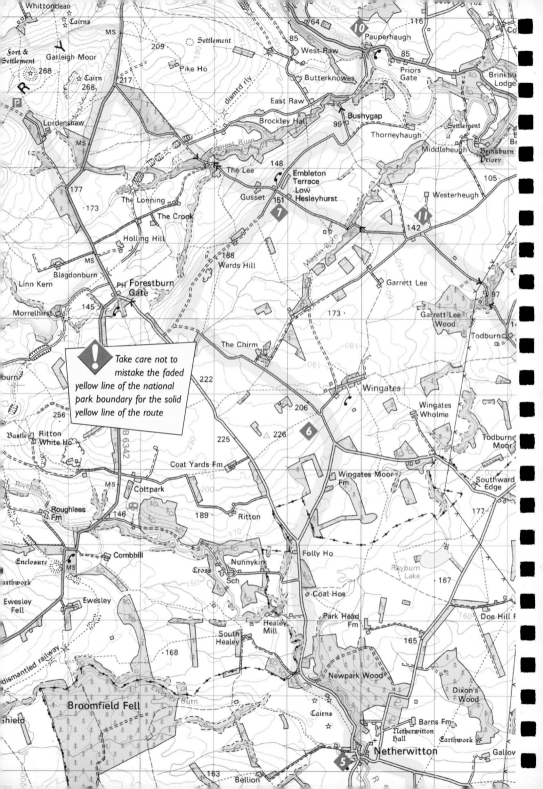

Take care not to mistake the faded yellow line of the national park boundary for the solid yellow line of the route

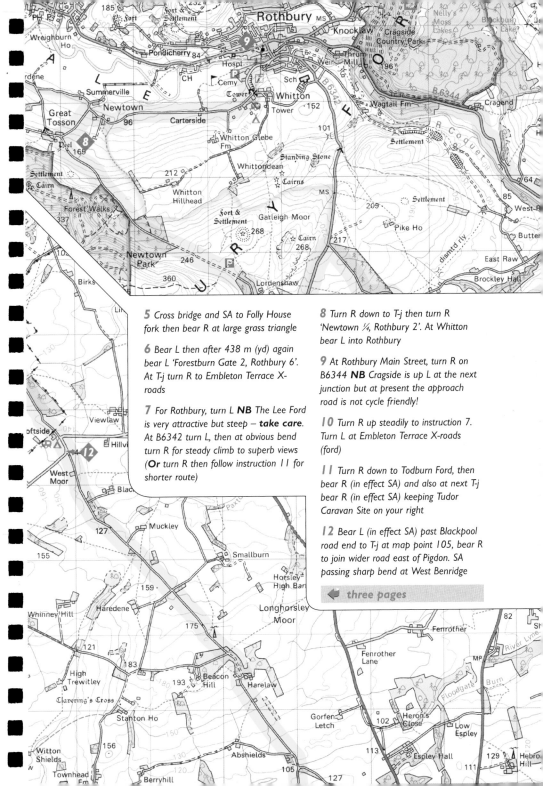

5 Cross bridge and SA to Folly House fork then bear R at large grass triangle

6 Bear L then after 438 m (yd) again bear L 'Forestburn Gate 2, Rothbury 6'. At T-j turn R to Embleton Terrace X-roads

7 For Rothbury, turn L **NB** The Lee Ford is very attractive but steep – **take care**. At B6342 turn L, then at obvious bend turn R for steady climb to superb views (**Or** turn R then follow instruction 11 for shorter route)

8 Turn R down to T-j then turn R 'Newtown ¼, Rothbury 2'. At Whitton bear L into Rothbury

9 At Rothbury Main Street, turn R on B6344 **NB** Cragside is up L at the next junction but at present the approach road is not cycle friendly!

10 Turn R up steadily to instruction 7. Turn L at Embleton Terrace X-roads (ford)

11 Turn R down to Todburn Ford, then bear R (in effect SA) and also at next T-j bear R (in effect SA) keeping Tudor Caravan Site on your right

12 Bear L (in effect SA) past Blackpool road end to T-j at map point 105, bear R to join wider road east of Pigdon. SA passing sharp bend at West Benridge

◀ three pages

10 A coastal circuit from Alnwick via Warkworth and Alnmouth

Start

B1340 north of Alnwick

P Next to B1340, north of Alnwick, before slip road to A1 (GR 200143)

Distance and grade

59 km (37 miles) – short route 35 km (22 miles)

🚲🚲🚲 Moderate

Terrain

Whilst there are no serious hills, this ride does involve a limited amount of gentle ascent on the southern loop. The remaining sections are either reasonably level or downhill. Highest point – Hillhead, Shilbottle 172 m (564 ft). Lowest points – sea level

Nearest railway

Alnmouth, on the route

This ride takes in some of the highlights of Northumberland's coast and threads them together by means of quiet roads and country lanes. Warkworth and Alnmouth are as attractive as they are different; Craster has a special charm of its own and there is not one metre of the entire length of coastline connecting all three places that is less than mag-nificent. South and up from Alnwick to Shilbottle through pleasant countryside before curving back north to the picture-postcard large village/small town of Warkworth, which is dominated by its castle. The route turns inland and gently climbs back towards Shilbottle before descending into the old seaside port of Alnmouth with its tidal harbour and now tiny fishing fleet. On past traditional Northumbrian fishing cobles to Boulmer, then once more inland via Longhoughton and Howick Hall to return to the sea again at Craster before minor roads lead back to Alnwick – the Northumberland coast at its best.

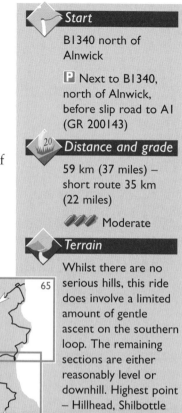

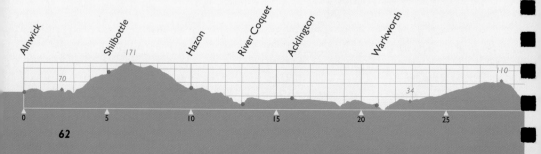

Warkworth 6

The town of the proud castle and the lowly hermitage set above the wooded banks of the River Coquet; a place where legends and myths merge with historical fact! The 14th-century hermitage and chapel, carved out of rock further upstream, is reputedly the finest in the country

Alnmouth 8

Built in 1150 and grew to become a significant North East sea port; on the hill to the south, stands the cross of St Cuthbert but the nearby Norman church of St Waleric was finally blown away on Christmas Day 1806 when a storm changed the course of the River Aln and cut off the site from the town. Warkworth/Alnmouth dunes and expansive beaches are clean, open and sandy

Craster 11

Picturesque fishing village with a tiny harbour built in 1906 by the Craster family in memory of a brother who died on active service in Tibet; now famous for Craster kippers (smoked herring). Dunstanburgh Castle stands in isolated splendour along the cliffs to the north. Cullernose Point, complete with guillimot colony teetering and swooping on white-washed basalt ledges, is well worth stopping for

▶ The River Coquet and Warkworth Castle

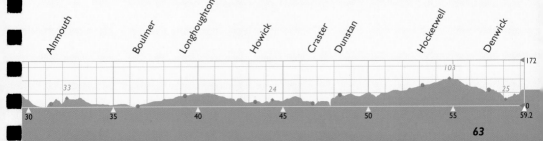

1 Up B1340 to Alnwick and turn L at the monument, then next R 'Swimming Pool, Sports Centre'. Residential road to Alnwick RFC; at roundabout turn L down Willowburn Ave to pass under A1 then turn R 'Shilbottle 2½'

➡ **two pages**

8 SA to Foxbury fork and turn R 'Boulmer, Longhoughton'. Sharp turn L to Longhoughton

9 Turn R 'North End' and keep R at obvious bend (point 49) then Bear R (in effect SA) 'Howick 1¼, Craster 3'

10 Turn L 'Howick' (red reflectors on fence) then at T-j turn L 'Craster 2' to X-roads

11 Turn R to Craster/ Dunstanburgh Castle, then retrace to X-roads via Dunstan. After PH bear L 'Alnwick 6¾'. Turn R 'Alnwick 6½' and SA at next cross-roads 'Alnwick 4½' to Hocketwell

12 Turn L 'Longhoughton 2¼, Howick 4, Lesbury 4'

13 Turn R 'Denwick 1½, Alnwick 4' (**NB** Limekilns in field on right and magnificent beech trees). At T-j turn R (NS) and at B1340 bear L to return to the start or into Alnwick

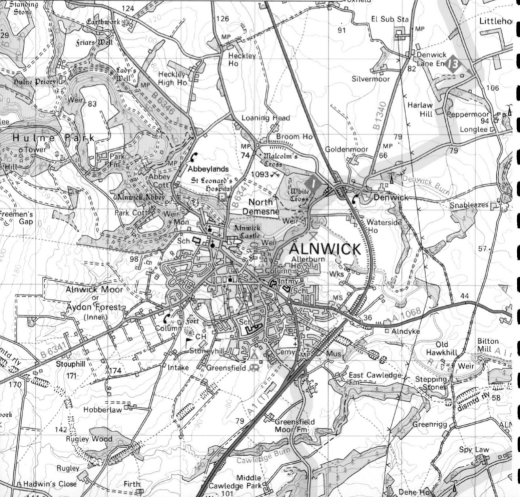

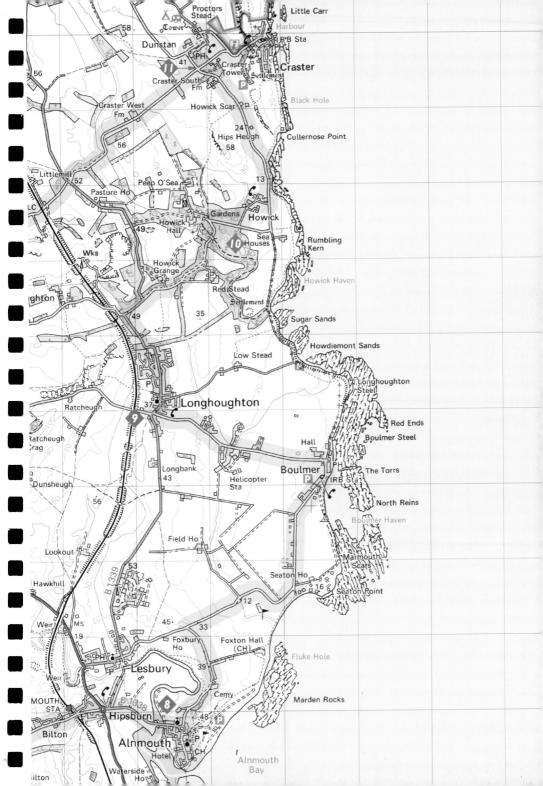

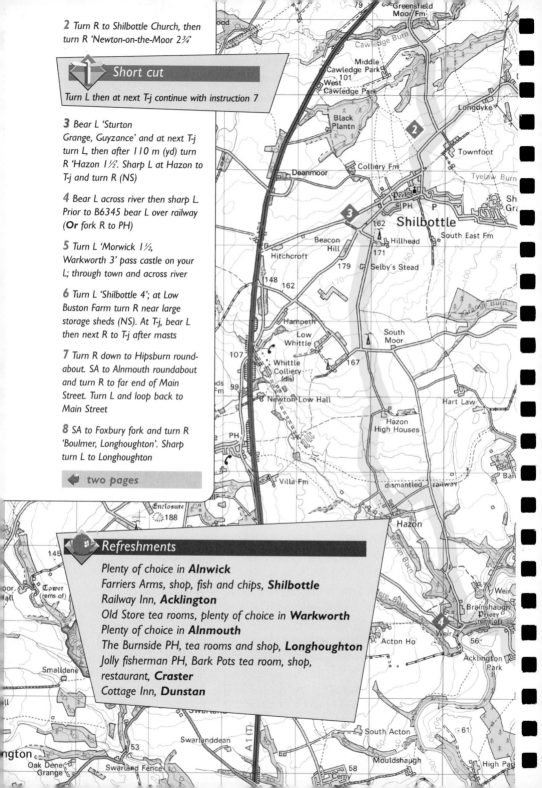

2 Turn R to Shilbottle Church, then turn R 'Newton-on-the-Moor 2¾'

↑ **Short cut**

Turn L then at next T-j continue with instruction 7

3 Bear L 'Sturton Grange, Guyzance' and at next T-j turn L, then after 110 m (yd) turn R 'Hazon 1½. Sharp L at Hazon to T-j and turn R (NS)

4 Bear L across river then sharp L. Prior to B6345 bear L over railway (**Or** fork R to PH)

5 Turn L 'Morwick 1½, Warkworth 3' pass castle on your L; through town and across river

6 Turn L 'Shilbottle 4'; at Low Buston Farm turn R near large storage sheds (NS). At T-j, bear L then next R to T-j after masts

7 Turn R down to Hipsburn roundabout. SA to Alnmouth roundabout and turn R to far end of Main Street. Turn L and loop back to Main Street

8 SA to Foxbury fork and turn R 'Boulmer, Longhoughton'. Sharp turn L to Longhoughton

← **two pages**

Refreshments

Plenty of choice in **Alnwick**
Farriers Arms, shop, fish and chips, **Shilbottle**
Railway Inn, **Acklington**
Old Store tea rooms, plenty of choice in **Warkworth**
Plenty of choice in **Alnmouth**
The Burnside PH, tea rooms and shop, **Longhoughton**
Jolly fisherman PH, Bark Pots tea room, shop, restaurant, **Craster**
Cottage Inn, **Dunstan**

West of Alnwick, through the Vale of Whittingham

Start

Prudhoe Road, Alnwick

P Next to B1340, north of Alnwick, before slip road to A1 (GR 200143)

20 Distance and grade

67 km (42 miles) – short route 46 km (29 miles)

/// Moderate

Terrain

Many kilometres of easy cycling inter-spersed with several hills – the downhills more than compen-sate. Highest point – Yetlington 200 m (656 ft). Lowest point – Alnwick 29 m (96 ft)

Nearest railway

Alnmouth, 6½ km (4 miles) east of the route

Alnwick lies on a cross-roads of long, straight highways, which, although they exist for historical reasons, do not generally aid the route planner. Nevertheless, as a base for cycle touring, Alnwick has much to commend it and the hills that shelter the county town on its western flank are not a serious proposition given some ingenuity and a decent breakfast. The climb out of Alnwick does not go on forever and is soon forgotten as the views of the route ahead beckon and entice. The rewarding descent through Bolton and on into the Vale of Whittingham is a portent of the quiet lanes and magnificent countryside that lie ahead. After a stop in picturesque Whittingham, continue on past Callaly with its magnificent tall beeches and wend your way pleasantly on to just north of Powburn. The route follows yet more rural roads to the attrac-tive village of Eglingham and two short detours minimise the use of the relatively quiet road back into Alnwick.

Alnwick 1

Rich in heritage, steeped in history and overflowing in character, the walled town of Alnwick, pronounced 'Annick', with its imposing gateways, is the county town of Northumberland. It is the domain of the House of Percy and the magnificent castle dominates the town and its past

The Vale of Whittingham 4

Charming village astride the narrow River Aln and was once an important staging post on the Newcastle to Edinburgh road set in the midst of a wide, flat valley. The Whittingham Sword, pronounced 'Whittingjum', was discovered in c.1850 and pre-dates 550 BC

Eglingham 8

Pronounced 'Eglingjum', a pretty little village with an interesting past; a nearby ancient earthwork called the Ringses, Eglingham Hall built on the site of an old peel tower where Cromwell once spent the night then quarrelled next morning with his host Henry Ogle. The exceptionally long church was built on a site granted to the monastery of Lindisfarne in 738 by King Coelwulf

▶ *The River Aln and Alnwick Castle*

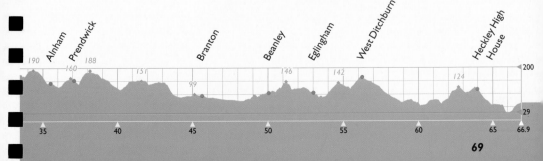

1 With the bus station down R, turn L up B6341. After 765 m (yd) turn L keeping Golf Course on your L, then on to T-j turn R to X-roads; turn R to B6341

2 Turn R for 328 m (yd) (path) then L. Turn next R over ford (bridge) to X-roads

3 Turn L, then SA at Bolton to next L and on to A697 X-roads

4 Take care – SA, at next T-j turn L into Whittingham. Turn 2nd R to T-j at Callaly

➡ *three pages*

10 SA to fork (grass triangle) bear L 'Eglingham 2¾'. **NB** Stone dovecote on the left

11 At T-j turn R, then bear L after 765 m (yd) to 'West Ditchburn 1¾'. Turn sharp R to rejoin B6346

12 Turn R for 5 km (3 miles), then SA to T-j above Heckley High House Farm. Turn R back to B6346

13 Turn L to return to Alnwick and the start

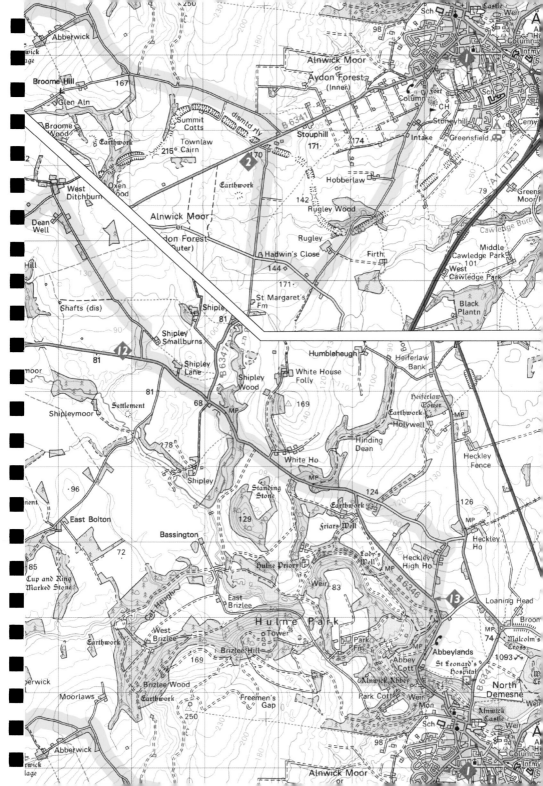

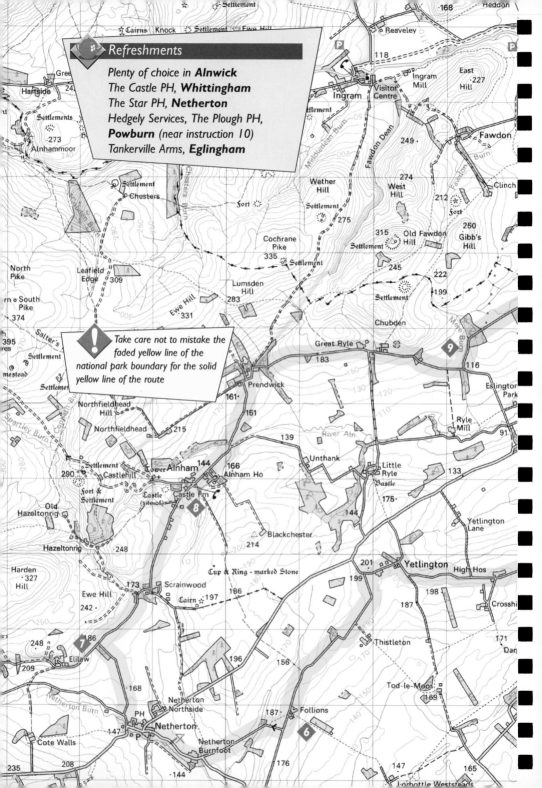

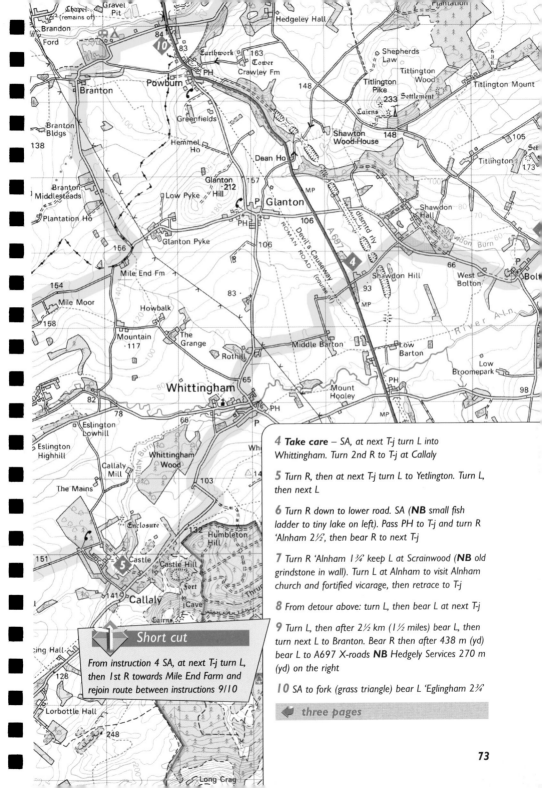

4 Take care – SA, at next T-j turn L into Whittingham. Turn 2nd R to T-j at Callaly

5 Turn R, then at next T-j turn L to Yetlington. Turn L, then next L

6 Turn R down to lower road. SA (**NB** small fish ladder to tiny lake on left). Pass PH to T-j and turn R 'Alnham 2½', then bear R to next T-j

7 Turn R 'Alnham 1¾' keep L at Scrainwood (**NB** old grindstone in wall). Turn L at Alnham to visit Alnham church and fortified vicarage, then retrace to T-j

8 From detour above: turn L, then bear L at next T-j

9 Turn L, then after 2½ km (1½ miles) bear L, then turn next L to Branton. Bear R then after 438 m (yd) bear L to A697 X-roads **NB** Hedgely Services 270 m (yd) on the right

10 SA to fork (grass triangle) bear L 'Eglingham 2¾'

◀ three pages

Short cut

From instruction 4 SA, at next T-j turn L, then 1st R towards Mile End Farm and rejoin route between instructions 9/10

From Belford to Seahouses, returning over Chatton Moor

In the not too distant future, it should be possible to cross the A1 at Belford by means of a new bridge built especially for non-motorised users. This ride is split down the middle by the A1, which, being a major trunk road, has precious few safe crossing points. Fortuitously, our second crossing takes advantage of the ideally placed under-pass at North Charlton, which links up directly with the lovely Hepburn Moor road. The route has two distinct characteristics: the eastern half takes advantage of the coastal plain and is almost totally devoid of any significant hills on its way to proud Bamburgh and scenic Seahouses; the western half provides a contrasting experience over glorious moorland with outstanding views of the rolling Cheviot Hills. Chillingham Castle and estate add stately grandeur and the final climb out of Chatton soon pales as the reward of exceptional coastal views is repaid in plenty.

Start

The centre of Belford

🅿 On the B6349, west end of Belford

Distance and grade

54 km (34 miles)

🌢🌢🌢 Moderate

Terrain

A long, gentle climb to Hepburn Moor with steep descent; one further climb near Chatton Park, then downhill to the start. Highest point – Hepburn Moor 253 m (830 ft); Lowest point – 7 m (26 ft)

Nearest railway

Berwick-upon-Tweed, 24 km (15 miles) north of the route

Bamburgh 4

Magnificent castle in a beautiful setting; old-fashioned village clustered round a wooded green and a stormy history spanning 14 centuries. Miles of superb beaches and sand dunes, fine views of the Farne Islands – a place to stir the imagination and well worth a longer *sojourn*. Legends abound such as the Spindlestone Dragon or Laidley Worm (loathsome snake or serpent) but the heroism of Grace Darling takes pride of place; her life, which was centred on Bamburgh and the Farne Islands, is commemorated in the museum

Seahouses 5

Long established fishing port with busy harbour and 18th-century limekilns, now suffering an identity crisis with the introduction of seaside amusements, yet the traditional ways of 'the harvest of the sea' refuse to give way to modern trends. You can book a boat trip to see the Farne Islands, which is a must; June is best but (seriously) wear warm clothes and wear a hat!

Chillingham 10

The ancestral home of the Earl of Tankerville and the 800-year home of the Chillingham Wild Cattle; sole survivors of their species remaining pure and uncrossed with any domestic cattle, always breeding white calves and totally unique

▲ *Seahouses*

Refreshments

'Singin' Hinny tea rooms, various in **Belford**
Copper Kettle tea rooms, various in **Bamburgh**
Plenty of choice in **Seahouses**
The Packhorse PH, **Ellingham**
Mason's Arms PH, Little Chef, **North Charlton**
Percy Arms PH, **Chatton**

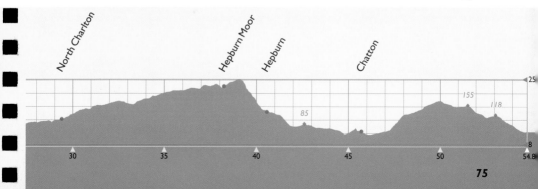

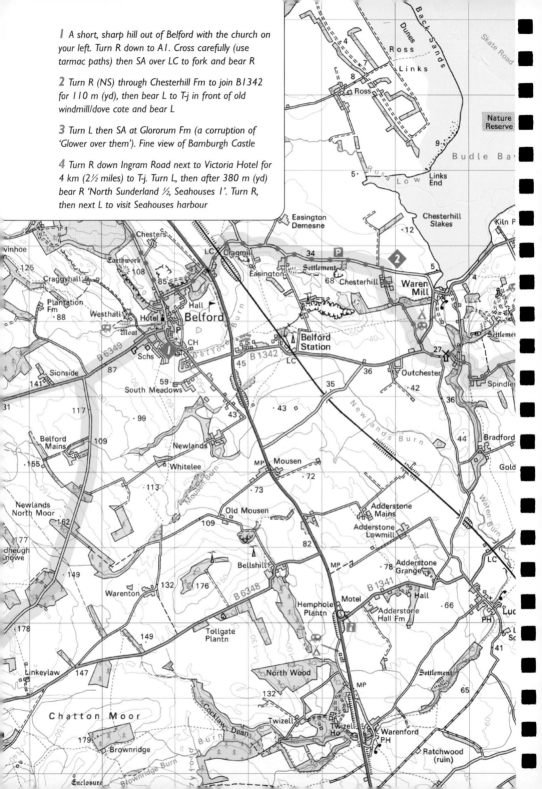

1 A short, sharp hill out of Belford with the church on your left. Turn R down to A1. Cross carefully (use tarmac paths) then SA over LC to fork and bear R

2 Turn R (NS) through Chesterhill Fm to join B1342 for 110 m (yd), then bear L to T-j in front of old windmill/dove cote and bear L

3 Turn L then SA at Glororum Fm (a corruption of 'Glower over them'). Fine view of Bamburgh Castle

4 Turn R down Ingram Road next to Victoria Hotel for 4 km (2½ miles) to T-j. Turn L, then after 380 m (yd) bear R 'North Sunderland ½, Seahouses 1'. Turn R, then next L to visit Seahouses harbour

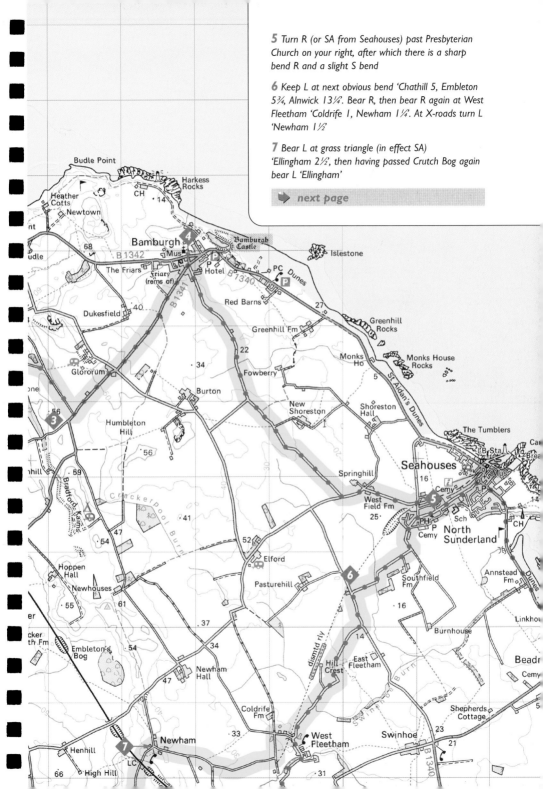

5 Turn R (or SA from Seahouses) past Presbyterian Church on your right, after which there is a sharp bend R and a slight S bend

6 Keep L at next obvious bend 'Chathill 5, Embleton 5¾, Alnwick 13¼'. Bear R, then bear R again at West Fleetham 'Coldrife 1, Newham 1¼'. At X-roads turn L 'Newham 1½'

7 Bear L at grass triangle (in effect SA) 'Ellingham 2½', then having passed Crutch Bog again bear L 'Ellingham'

➡ next page

7 Bear L at grass triangle (in effect SA) 'Ellingham 2½', then having passed Crutch Bog again bear L 'Ellingham'

8 Turn R at PH (NS), then bear R 'Belford 8, Alnwick 8, North Charlton 2'. SA at X-roads 'Doxford Hall 1½' (farm vegetables sign), then bear R along private road (bridleway) to pass under the A1

9 (Turn R for refreshments.) Turn L, then R 'Chillingham' to enjoy 11 km (7 miles) of Northumberland at its best! 1:8 descent needs care.

10 Turn R past Chillingham to Chatton and turn R through village (PH). Cross bridge

11 Turn L 'Belford 4' to B6349, then turn R to return to the start

◀ two pages

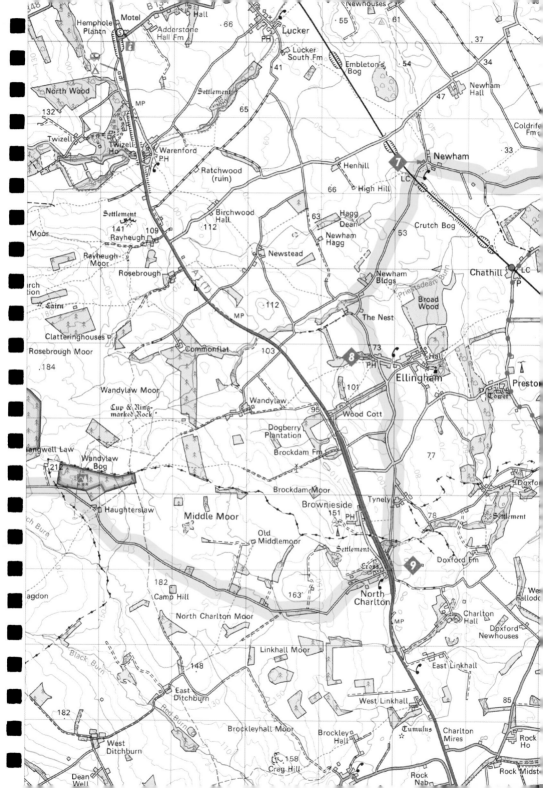

13 *A circuit of the Kyloe Hills and a visit to Holy Island*

Belford is an ideal location for a number of excellent cycle tours that are just waiting to be enjoyed in this area. It is well placed for access to the coast as well as the fine Northumberland countryside that lies inland. This tour is reasonably short but visits one of the most evocative places in the UK. After the initial climb up Belford Moor, from which the ever-present panoramic views extend in all directions, the lovely Kyloe Hills are rounded on their western flank to reach the causeway road to Lindisfarne (or Holy Island). The 'cradle of Christianity' will not disappoint and is well worth exploring but do not underestimate the time, distance and energy for the return cycle to the mainland. The now reasonably quiet section past Middleton Hall is wide and straight, being part of the old A1, and offers fine coastal views – all of which serve to make the circuit a most enjoyable experience.

Start

The centre of Belford

P On the B6349, west end of Belford

20 Distance and grade

48 km (30 miles) – short distance to allow for the tide and time on the Island

Easy

Terrain

Apart from the initial climb over Belford Moor, the route is either flat or downhill. Highest point – approaching Belford Moor 178 m (584 ft). Lowest point – sea level

Nearest railway

Berwick-upon-Tweed 14 km (9 miles) from the route

84   85

Belford

82   83

▶ *Lindisfarne Castle, Holy Island*

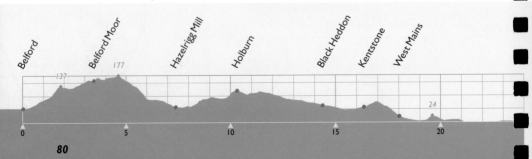

Belford   Belford Moor 137   177   Hazelrigg Mill   Holburn   Black Heddon   Kentstone   West Mains 24

0   5   10   15   20

Belford 1

Once busy little town/large village on the old main road to Edinburgh; irregular streets and grey-stone houses built on a gradual slope that steepens to the north. 18th-century Belford Hall is close to the town; the old market cross marks the centre of a thriving community during the Middle Ages

Lindisfarne or Holy Island

Unique island with holy memories lying over a kilometre (¾ mile) off the Northumberland coast and cut off twice daily by the tide but connected by tarmac causeway with refuge. Do not attempt to race the tide and be alert to traffic flow that mirrors tidal flow. Lindisfarne Priory dates back to 1100 and the whole island is sacred ground hallowed by its links with St Aidan and St Cuthbert. Lindisfarne Castle sits on top of a conicle-shaped, dolerite rock tower; the harbour and coastal areas are particularly picturesque

Refreshments

Singin' Hinny Tea Rooms,
various, **Belford**
The Plough PH, A11/**Beal Road**
Various in **Lindisfarne**

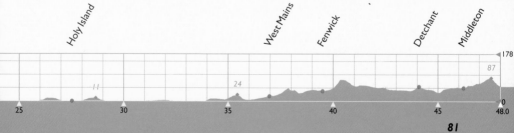

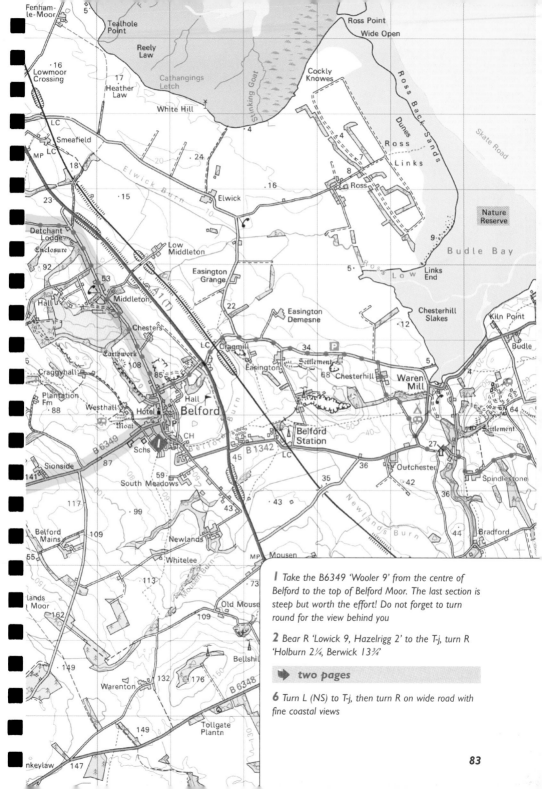

1 Take the B6349 'Wooler 9' from the centre of Belford to the top of Belford Moor. The last section is steep but worth the effort! Do not forget to turn round for the view behind you

2 Bear R 'Lowick 9, Hazelrigg 2' to the T-j, turn R 'Holburn 2¼, Berwick 13¾'

➡ **two pages**

6 Turn L (NS) to T-j, then turn R on wide road with fine coastal views

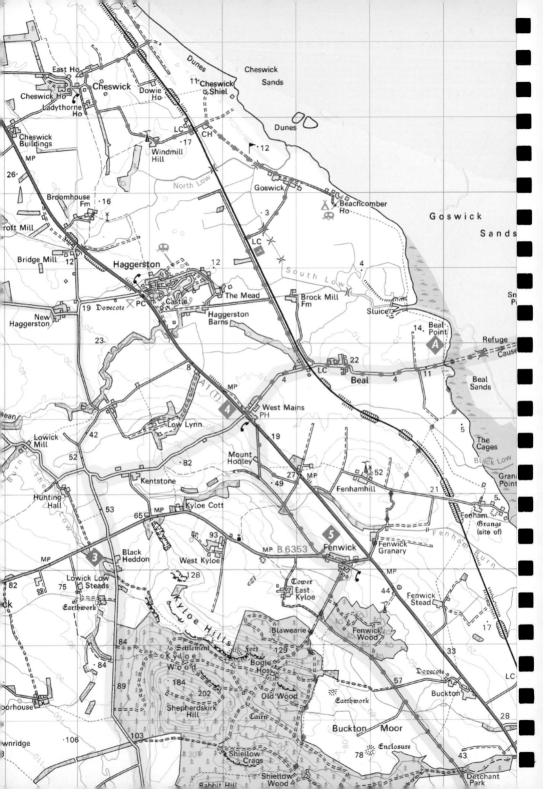

3 At B6353 X-roads SA to T-j, then turn R 'Kentstone, Beal' to A I

4 Cross carefully, then turn R. Turn L along short section of old road past the garage for a further 55 m (yd) using the wide grass verge until opposite the minor road **NB** new crossing point planned. Cross carefully, then narrow road

to B6353. (**Or** SA, tide tables on the left, shop at garage and PH **NB** The causeway access road can be busy as the traffic flows in time with the tide)

A **Take care.** Check the tide times before crossing and **allow plenty of time.** Remember your return across the causeway

may be against a headwind. Retrace to instruction 4

5 Bear L then bear R at Fenwick leading to a short, sharp hill. Bear L to free-wheel almost all of the way to Detchant

two pages

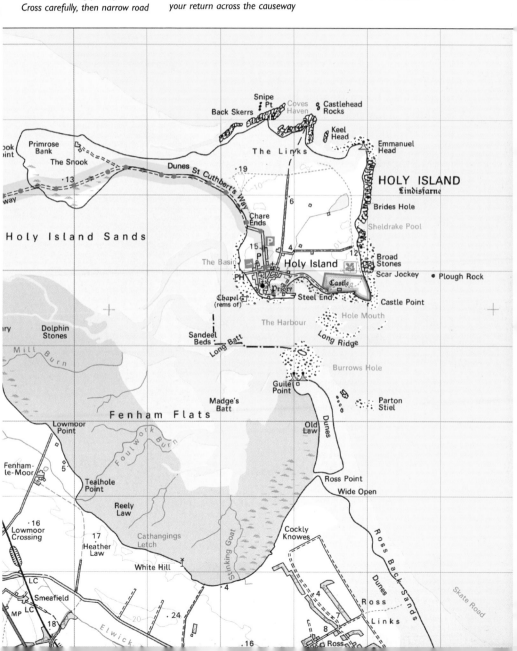

A circuit from Bishop Auckland on railway paths, and quiet lanes

At the present time, there are some 120 km (75 miles) of converted railway paths in County Durham with proposals for more to be added when finance becomes available. This ride follows two separate but converging railway paths, a very pleasant minor road and a section of linking bridleways – most of which are situated in a truly rural setting. The ride starts and finishes at Bishop Auckland for convenience but can be joined at any point. The Auckland Walk links with Spennymoor of which little is seen. The ensuing bridleways add an interesting off-road aspect to the circuit, then a quiet, minor road leads to the Brandon/Bishop Auckland Walk. Finally, the Newton Cap Viaduct provides the high-level river crossing to return to the start.

 Start

Bishop Auckland, near Auckland Castle

P Parking by the river at Bishop Auckland (GR 213303); short steep hill (Wear Chare) – take care joining the route

 Distance and grade

29 km (18 miles)

Easy

Terrain

All the railway paths are level and there is only one real hill on the entire route in the shape of a steady haul on the A689 to join the Auckland Walk railway path. Highest point – A689/railway path 141 m (463 ft). Lowest point – Sunderland Bridge 38 m (125 ft)

Nearest railway

Bishop Auckland

Refreshments

Plenty of choice in **Bishop Auckland**
Various off the route in **Spennymoor**
Various off the route in **Brandon**
Various in **Willington**

▲ *Brancepeth Castle near Brandon*

 Places of interest

Bishop Auckland 1
Small town of local importance with a mixture of old and new architecture; Auckland Castle had humble beginnings as a manor house but was converted into a castle in about 1300, which was the start of a long process of enlargements and alterations designed to beautify the place. Much was destroyed by fire in the 1650s and largely restored 10 years later; the residence of the Bishop of Durham since Norman times

Byers Green, Whitworth Hall and Bracepeth Castle
Byers Green Station (2) can still be seen; 'byers' means ancient woods that grew around the village. Whitworth Hall (west of 4) was once the home of the musical legend, Bobby Shaftoe. Brancepeth Castle (southwest of 10), much restored in the 19th century, was originally a 13th-century castle built by the Nevill family to replace a Saxon stronghold

Binchester 2/3
Roman military station on the Dere Street known as 'Vinovia', which means pleasant place; the hypercaust is the best example of a Roman bath house in Britain. NB Off-route, but a picturesque, minor road along the River Wear will add pleasure to a worthwhile detour

Scripton
Brancepeth
Willington
119
99 124
89
141
38
15
20
25
28.7

1 Ascend Wear Chare, then turn L to pass the main entrance to Auckland Castle on your left. Descend A689 all too briefly, then ascend all too slowly to railway path which passes under the road

2 Descend to railway path on south side of road, then turn L

3 Turn L, then next R to Tudhoe Grange Estate. Turn L to corner of estate

4 Bear R keeping houses on your right and follow path through wood, down to stream

5 Cross concrete bridge, then up and around L to minor road, turn R

6 Turn L, then sharp R (bridleway) to farm track. SA along field edge (narrow) to corner of wood

7 Enter wood (tricky) and follow path (can be muddy) down to stream (awkward bridge)

8 Keep river on your left and follow improving track to old Sunderland Bridge. Turn L, then sharp L along obvious track keeping river on your left

9 Bear L to join minor road, then turn R to A690. Turn R, then sharp L to railway path

10 Turn L and follow railway path to Newton Cap Viaduct (A689/Bishop Auckland)

11 Cross bridge using footpath, then turn L to return to the start

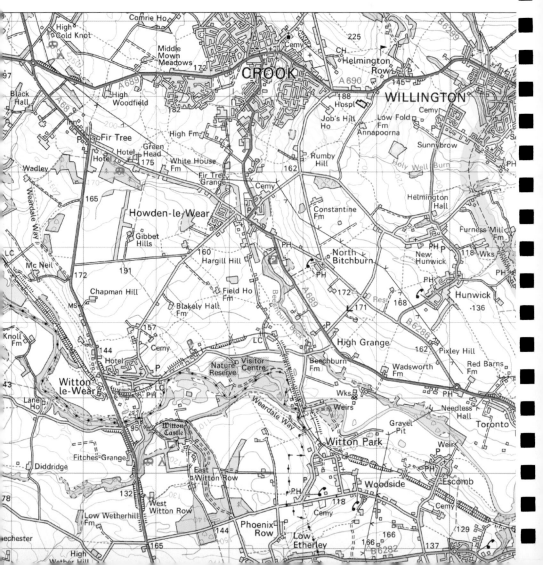

East of Washington around Penshaw Monument

One of the possible destinations of the C2C Cycle Route is Sunderland and this ride uses its west/east axis, albeit in the opposite direction, to form the longest side of the circuit. Surrounded by conurbations, this surprisingly rural ride can be joined at any point but starts near Rickleton for convenience. A bridleway leads close to Lambton Castle, then links with light-controlled Biddick Bridge across the river Wear before passing under the A182 and through Biddick Woods via Boundary Houses and south of Success to Philadelphia and on to New Herrington. Bridleways connect West and Middle Herrington, after which Foxcover Road leads to Offerton Lane and the C2C route. Cox Green pedestrian bridge gives pleasant access to North Biddick and leaving the excellent railway path at Vigo Wood, the path through Rickleton completes the enjoyably rural circuit of Penshaw Monument.

Start

Bonemill Lane, near Rickleton (GR 294537)

P Parking at the Sports Ground midway along the south side of the road between Rickleton and Fatfield (Bonemill Lane)

Distance and grade

22 km (14 miles)

Easy

Terrain

Only one short uphill approaching instruction 7 but there are several good descents. Do the ride clockwise if you want more exercise! Highest point – approaching instruction 7 109 m (358 ft). Lowest point – sea level

Nearest railway

Chester-le-Street, 3 km (2 miles) southwest of the start

Refreshments

Plenty of choice in **Biddock area**
Shoulder of Mutton PH, **West Herrington**
Oddfellows Arms PH, **Cox Green**

Cox Green 10

The village of Cox Green and the settlement of Barmston on the opposite bank of the river shared three boat-building yards; two slipways are still visible. In days gone by, the main industries were boat-building, quarrying and river work; prior to 1955, a wire rope and rowing boat were the only means of crossing the river until the present bridge was built in 1958. Upstream from the bridge (south side) is Alice's Well, which still produces spring water; this was the only souce of drinking water until World War 2

Penshaw Monument 5

In 1840, it was decided to build a monument to the memory of the Earl of Durham who had just died. Penshaw Hill was selected and Penshaw Monument was built in the design of a Grecian temple based on the temple of Theseus. Watched by a crowd of over 10,000 people, the foundation stone was laid in 1844; the 21 m (70 ft) high monument, which is a highly visible landmark, is now owned by the National Trust. Its main claim to fame is that the legendary Lambton Worm wrapped its tail ' 10 times round Penshaw Hill'

▲ *Washington Old Hall, Washington*

1 Leave Bonemill Lane with the Sports Fields on your right (bridleway). Follow tarmac road under A182, then on to cross Biddick Bridge

2 Turn R down cul-de-sac between houses (bridleway) to pass under the A182

3 Cross over to tarmac path and turn L over bridge. Take next turn R after 30 mph sign (Briar Lea), then at T-j turn L (Bowes Lea). Take 2nd turn R, then through corner gap to access sports field and the road beyond. Turn R

4 Turn L alongside disused railway line to Philadelphia. Turn R, then sharp L **NB** old converted engine sheds. Through gap, then turn R (bridleway) keeping grass on your left. **NB** Site of Dorothea Pit

5 Under bridge, then onto tarmac road on right of railway path to sharp turn R by double row of red brick houses to West Herrington

6 SA with PH on the left to cross A19 (bridge), then turn L along Foxcover Road

7 SA, then turn R through Offerton and follow Offerton Lane parallel to, but separate from, the A19

8 Join Consett and Sunderland Railway Path (C2C) and turn L

9 Turn R down to River Wear, then turn L to cross bridge **NB** Alice Well in wall 33 m (yd) beyond bridge (south side)

10 Turn L (grass), then at 2nd seat turn R (clump of trees) past metal barrier to tarmac road and turn L to Jubilee Terrace. Turn R at near end (bridleway, 'Pattinson Pond'). Follow C2C Route signs in reverse. After next barrier turn L for 545 m (yd), then bear L under railway. **Easy to miss.** Immediate turn R to main railway path beyond burgundy coloured access control point

11 Bear L along Consett and Sunderland Railway Path crossing A182 to turn off L, midway between 2 sets of meter-high posts (red), in middle of track

12 Turn R on estate road to far end of houses. Turn L (Woodland Trust sign) and push your bike along the tarmac path to cross road at Rickleton Chapel to access sports field. Turn R and push your bike along the tarmac path until it passes under Bonemill Lane to the return to the start

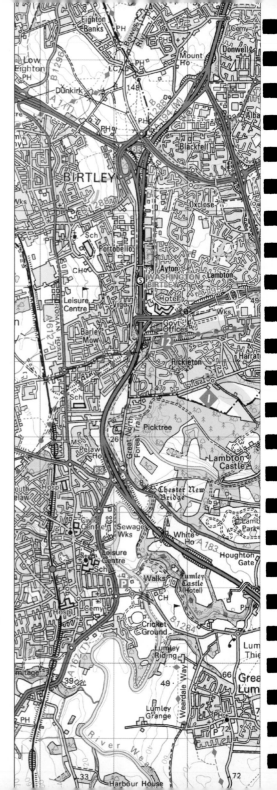

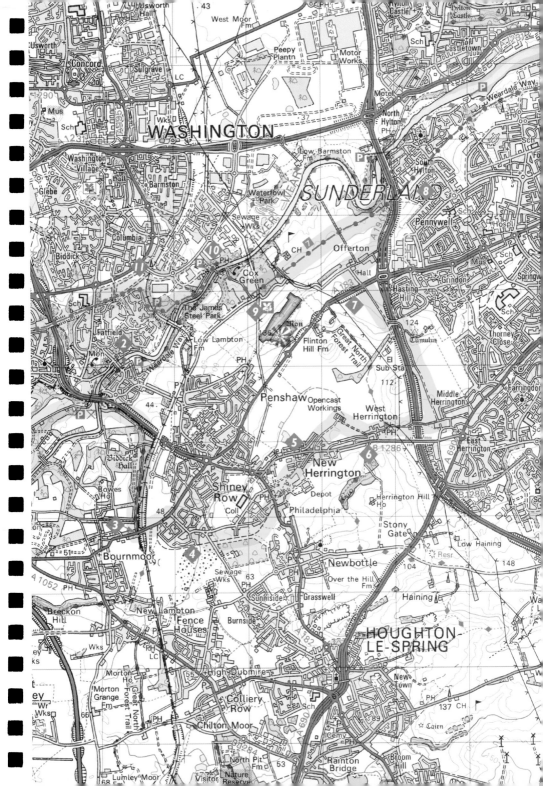

3 Along the Tyne from Prudhoe then southwest from Wylam

Commencing at the Tyne Riverside Country Park, this route goes through a short but enjoyable section before heading up and away from the riverside to cross the A695 and continue along very pleasant lanes to cross the Stanley Burn back into Northumberland. Once the Dukeshagg Bank is surmounted, the minor road beyond descends to connect with a very interesting bridleway heading west to a point where the route splits. The shorter option offers extremely rewarding views over Stocksfield Burn towards Broomley and Healey and the longer option provides an enjoyable and easy, rural ride. Both options merge at New Ridley just in time for the ascension to High Mickley. The descent via Cherryburn links up with a delightful lane that leads back to the A695 and the final descent to the country park.

Start

Tyne Riverside Country Park, Low Prudhoe (GR 086634)

P As above

Distance and grade

38 km (24 miles) – short route 26 km (16 miles)

🚵🚵🚵🚵 Moderate/ strenuous

🚵🚵🚵 Moderate short route

Terrain

Largely uses gravity to best advantage but there has to be height gain in order to enjoy the descents! The short-cut is a steady uphill track. Highest point – Currock Hill 249 m (817 ft). Lowest point – sea level, near Wylam

Nearest railway

Prudhoe

Prudhoe   Wylam   Currock Hill   Whittonstall
223
62
23
0   5   10   15

Refreshments

PH, **Prudhoe**
Bridge End PH, White
Swan PH, **Ovingham**
Various in **Wylam**
The Anchor PH ,
Whittonstall
Dr Syntax PH,
New Ridley
The Bluebell PH, **Low
Mickley** (off-route)
Jiggery Pokery tea rooms
Mickley Square

Places of interest

Prudhoe Castle /
Pronounced 'Pruda' and proudly standing on high ground to the south of the River Tyne. Built in late Norman times by Ordinel de Umfraville, probably on the site of a wooden stronghold, became the property of the Percys some 150 years later. A magnificent castle with an interesting history and well worth a visit

The Spetchells /
Lying next to the cycle path are the Spetchells, which are long, large heaps of white lime. Originally stockpiled for later distribution to farms for the purpose of neutralising acidic land, thus encouraging optimum growth potential, the heaps have become well-established landmarks

◀ George
Stephenson's Cottage,
Wylam

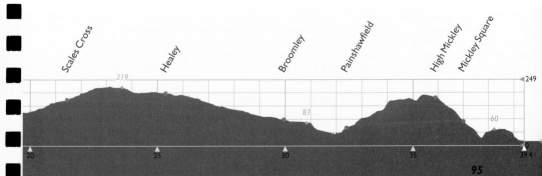

95

1 Under the Ovingham metal bridge with the River Tyne on your L. Turn L before railway bridge at end of cottages to cross West Wylam Bridge

2 Through car park, then turn L across river and LC. Along Station Road around bend, then bear R at small triangle 'Sled Road, Bradley Hall Gardens and Nurseries'

3 Turn R (footpath), then bear R on old road 'Bradley Hall, Access Only' to gap on left (traffic lights/cattle crossing point). Straight over (**take care**), cattle grid

4 Tarmac ends, bear L to next fork, then bear R across Stanley Burn. At minor road turn L up to farm, then on to X-roads

5 SA down to T-j and turn L to wide corner. Bear R to Hollings Fm (bridleway) 'Cockshot Hill 1¾'. SA at farm (normally, large bales make this section very narrow) then through field into wood. **NB** drift mine on right

6 At open, level ground turn L up short hill (good stone base), then on to X-roads. SA (**take care**) 'Unsuitable for HGVs'. At farm turn R (bridleway) next to fence, then turn L on minor road

7 Turn R 'Stocksfield 3¾ with good views of Simonsides in the distance. At T-j turn L **NB** 'The Lead Road' see wall inscription. 'Scales Cross 1¼, Slaley 3¾'

8 SA (**take care**), then after over 1 km (¾ mile) turn R on farm track 'Healey 1¼, High Fotherley ¾' (bridleway). After trees on left where track curves right turn L down grass track, then through wood on stone-based track

Short cut

SA to T-j, then turn L. At next bend SA on Permissive track with superb views. At T-j turn R

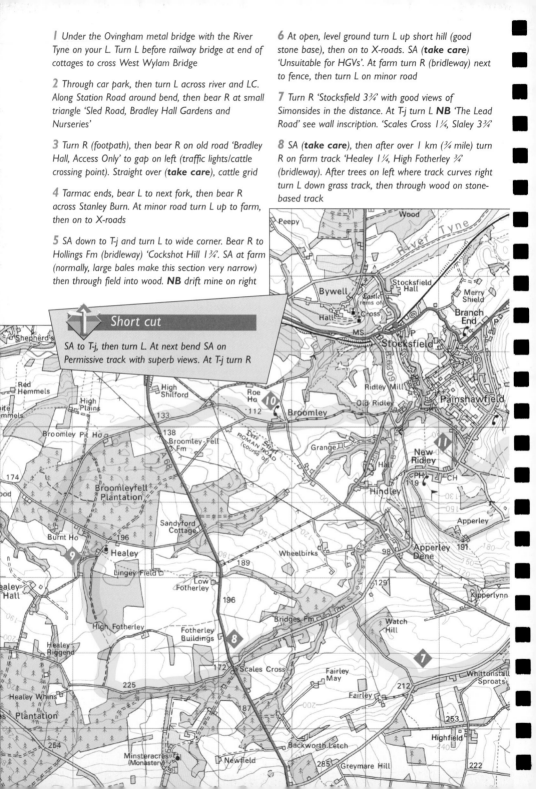

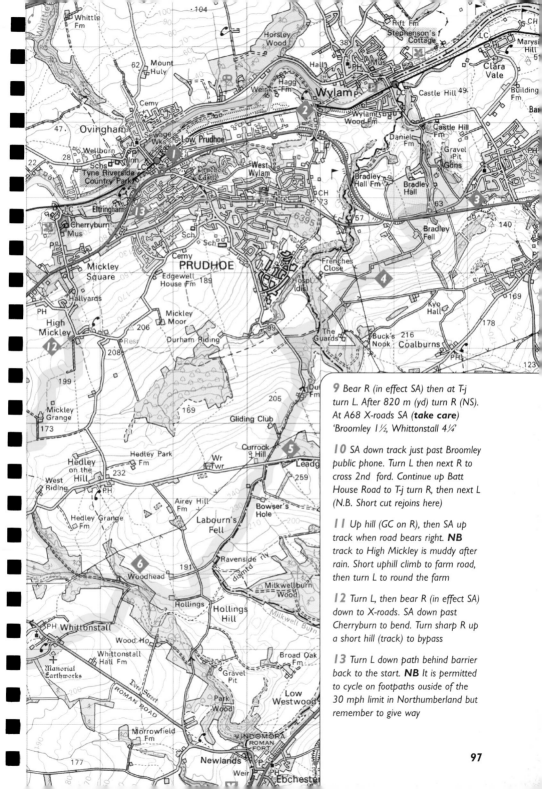

9 Bear R (in effect SA) then at T-j turn L. After 820 m (yd) turn R (NS). At A68 X-roads SA (**take care**) 'Broomley 1½, Whittonstall 4¼'

10 SA down track just past Broomley public phone. Turn L then next R to cross 2nd ford. Continue up Batt House Road to T-j turn R, then next L (N.B. Short cut rejoins here)

11 Up hill (GC on R), then SA up track when road bears right. **NB** track to High Mickley is muddy after rain. Short uphill climb to farm road, then turn L to round the farm

12 Turn L, then bear R (in effect SA) down to X-roads. SA down past Cherryburn to bend. Turn sharp R up a short hill (track) to bypass

13 Turn L down path behind barrier back to the start. **NB** It is permitted to cycle on footpaths ouside of the 30 mph limit in Northumberland but remember to give way

4 Across fells north of Bellingham and east to Linnheads Lake

This ride is an energetic excursion over a great variety of terrain. After gradually gaining height above Bellingham, the Pennine Way bridleway is followed as far as the quiet B6320 but the surface varies and requires care – during or after wet weather the on-road alternative is recommended. Choose a clear day to enjoy the wonderful views during the superb descent from Corsenside Common, now rarely used by the military. Two little-known bridges are revealed by dint of rarelyused Unclassified County Roads (UCRs) and are the 'hidden secrets' of the ride. East Woodburn Common leads past picturesque Linnheads Lake and then very pleasantly through the forest to access a short stretch of fell. The return route, threading past Sweethope Loughs, takes advantage of narrow tarmac with no shortage of views. There is an optional off-road link for those with boundless energy and rear suspension and the final loop, north of Redesmouth, should not be missed.

Start

Main Street, Bellingham (GR 839834)

P As above or on left beyond public toilets

Distance and grade

42 km (26 miles) – short route 24 km (15 miles)

///// Strenuous

//// Moderate/ strenuous short route

Terrain

A complete mix of terrain and surfaces; an amalgam of all that is good and challenging in an off-road ride. In general, the spectacular downs far outweigh the necessary ups.

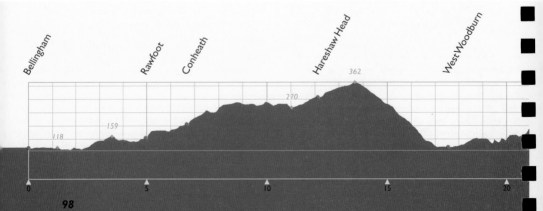

Highest point –
Corsenside Common
364 m (1194 ft).
Lowest point – Rede
Bridge 107 m (353 ft)

Nearest railway

Corbridge, 19 km
(12 miles) south of the
route

▲ *The Bellingham Gingall*

Refreshments

*Various, cafe and tea
rooms,* **Bellingham**
Bay Horse, shop,
West Woodburn

Places of interest

West Woodburn 9

Small village on the A68 close to the
great Roman road, Dere Street. The
route ran from York to Hadrian's Wall,
then continued northwards, actually
crossing the River Rede at the end of
instruction 8. Some of the stones
in the river were part of the original
bridge, built when the river used to
flood and became a lake before
upstream Catcleugh
Reservoir dam was con-
structed. Until AD 140, the
bridgehead was a small
island in the middle of a
swamp when the Romans
decided to build a fort
called Habitancum, now
known as Risingham.
Abandoned in about AD
367, the fort lay untouched
until 1822, when the site
was bought by the Shanks
family who John Hodgson,
the vicar and local historian,
later encouraged to excavate. In 1839,
John Shanks unearthed a cement-lined
bath, which was then destroyed to dis-
courage sightseers. Certain valuable
finds were sent to Newcastle including
the altar of local god Magons, and a
4th-century Christian tombstone

Hartside

Sweethope Loughs

Green Rigg

Buteland Fell

Rede Bridge

364

279

289

227

200

141

111

107

25

30

35

40

41.9

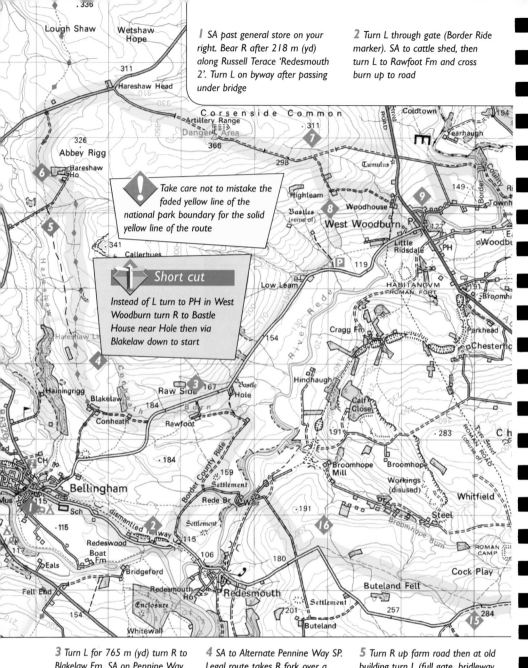

1 SA past general store on your right. Bear R after 218 m (yd) along Russell Terace 'Redesmouth 2'. Turn L on byway after passing under bridge

2 Turn L through gate (Border Ride marker). SA to cattle shed, then turn L to Rawfoot Fm and cross burn up to road

! Take care not to mistake the faded yellow line of the national park boundary for the solid yellow line of the route

Short cut

Instead of L turn to PH in West Woodburn turn R to Bastle House near Hole then via Blakelaw down to start

3 Turn L for 765 m (yd) turn R to Blakelaw Fm. SA on Pennine Way through farm to post on near horizon. SA to corner of wall, then up to post on next horizon – on the right of trees (gate)

4 SA to Alternate Pennine Way SP. Legal route takes R fork over a number of drainage ditches to wall by Scotch Pine, no gate. Turn L down wall to bottom gate, to meet Alternate Pennine Way

5 Turn R up farm road then at old building turn L (full gate, bridleway sign). Traverse (full gate) to red stream (iron deposits), bear R through gate and SA on double width track (old wagonway)

6 Turn R on B6320 to farm, then turn R again (public road – rarely closed for firing)

7 After descending past 2nd set of red warning signs on gate look for half bend in road then, after 218 m (yd), turn R (gate/stone posts) onto double rough track, downhill to farm

8 At gate keep L around farm to tarmac road (bridleway). Descend to Woodhouse. Turn R through gate past metal barn on double track to road. Turn L to PH in West Woodburn

9 16 m (yd) beyond PH (wide path) turn R, then L after 656 m (yd) up to corner. At gate turn R to Blackburn Bridge. Turn R

10 SA (gate) to double track. Track bends on up to gap in rocky skyline (with a quarry behind)

11 After 27 m (yd) bear R keeping wall on your right. Through end gate, keeping wall on left, to red track. SA across track, then after 165 m (yd) continue diagonally down to follow track into wood, lake on right

12 Bear R (look for small quarry on left). **Easy to miss**. Down to bend but SA on forest ride (fire gap) to bridle gate and to fell – walk this section

13 Follow fence, then cut diagonally down to old Wanney railway line – keep well left of small hut, through tunnel (near to trees) then up steeply (rideable!) and across to road

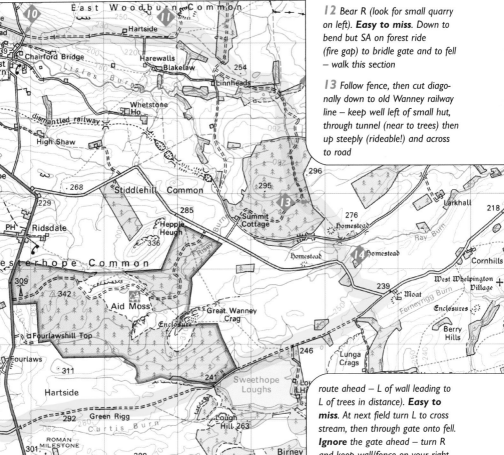

14 Turn L, then next R past lake **take care** – listen for following traffic – to A68 X-roads. SA (**take care**) 765 m (yd) to gate on right, just past small quarry on left. Continue SA on-road to

instruction 15 (and on-road to instruction 16 to miss next bumpy off-road section)

15 **Easy to miss**. Turn R on feint track to brow, then downhill (sight

route ahead – L of wall leading to L of trees in distance). **Easy to miss**. At next field turn L to cross stream, then through gate onto fell. **Ignore** the gate ahead – turn R and keep wall/fence on your right past wood. Continue diagonally to corner of field and onto road

16 SA, then R, after 330 m (yd) turn R down to Rede Bridge, then up to reverse first section back to the start

5 *Weaving along the Wansbeck, west of Morpeth*

*T*he wild and windy Wanneys lie to the west of this route and are a truly craggy domain. The Wansbeck has its source close by before it curls its way eastwards on a relatively short jouney to the sea. There are a total of eight river crossings on this ride, not counting the numerous burns or streams – the River Wansbeck alone is crossed five times over the first 9 km (5½ miles). The rivers Wansbeck, Font and Hart Burn have all joined forces by Mitford, but the map-bleary cyclist may be prone to river-confusion as the ride progresses. The route weaves its way around numerous hamlets, all whilst threading its way back and forth across the various water courses. By this means, and the use of rarely used unclassified County roads now little more than tracks, the route will take you into some of Northumberland's loveliest places. A network of quiet lanes leads easily and gently onto higher ground

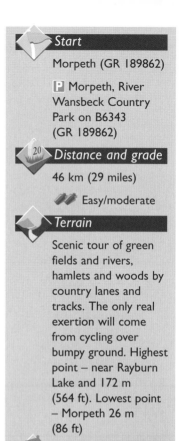

Start

Morpeth (GR 189862)

🅿 Morpeth, River Wansbeck Country Park on B6343 (GR 189862)

Distance and grade

46 km (29 miles)

Easy/moderate

Terrain

Scenic tour of green fields and rivers, hamlets and woods by country lanes and tracks. The only real exertion will come from cycling over bumpy ground. Highest point – near Rayburn Lake and 172 m (564 ft). Lowest point – Morpeth 26 m (86 ft)

Nearest railway

Morpeth

from which you can see the distant Simonside and Cheviot Hills. Beckon though they will, 'weaving along the Wansbeck' is the treat that this ride has in store.

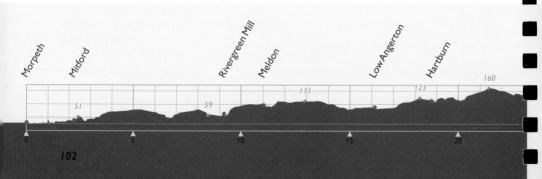

Morpeth and the Wansbeck Valley

Further to this chapter's introduction, a historical perspective can add to the appreciation of the true Wansbeck Valley, which extends about 3 km (2 miles) between Morpeth and Mitford. About 2½ km (1½ miles) from Morpeth is Newminster Abbey of which very little remains; it was almost identical to Fountains Abbey in Yorkshire and was founded by Cistercian monks in 1137. The estate was extensive, stretching from the source of the Wansbeck, up Coquetdale with fisheries on the Tyne and saltworks at the mouth of both the Blyth and the Coquet. High Stanners was named after the small stones and gravel on the margins of the river; Low Stanners was formerly a place of execution on the eastern outskirts of the town. Lady's Walk leads to Newminster and refers to the Virgin Mother; Lover's Walk ends in the sheltered haugh below the ruins

Refreshments

Plenty of choice in **Morpeth**
The Plough PH, **Mitford**
The Dyke Neuk PH,
north of instruction 5

▲ Morpeth Embankment on the River Wansbeck

103

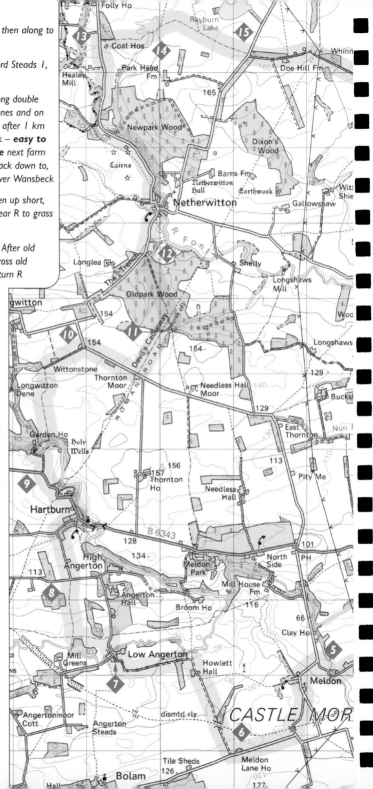

1 Cross bridge on B6343, then along to Mitford (PH)

2 Turn L 'Mitford ¼, Mitford Steads 1, Molesden 2½'

3 Turn R (in effect SA) along double track down to stepping stones and on up to B6343. Turn L, then after 1 km (¾ mile) turn L down track – **easy to miss** – 218 m (yd) **before** next farm on your right and follow track down to, and then alongside, the River Wansbeck

4 Cross narrow bridge, then up short, steep hill to minor road. Bear R to grass triangle

5 Turn L through Meldon. After old church on left bear R to cross old railway bridge to T-j, then turn R

6 Turn R through gate past Howlett Hall Fm, then sharp L to Low Angerton

7 SA, then through bridle gate on L (railway sleeper gatepost) just past wood on right. **NB** 'Causeway' across potential flood plain on right. Pass mature wood on right and cross field to gate with white Countryside Access sign (next to young wood on left). Turn R with fence on your right. Continue gently up to gate, then SA (easier) to road

8 SA 'Hartburn ¾', then bear R to Hartburn. Turn L at the cross

9 Turn R (in effect SA) over cattle grid, to cross River Wansbeck, then after 55 m (yd) bear R along narrow path/jungle (bridleway muddy after rain). Cross small stream (narrow bridge) and push up short, steep hill. Follow field edge to a better path near farm

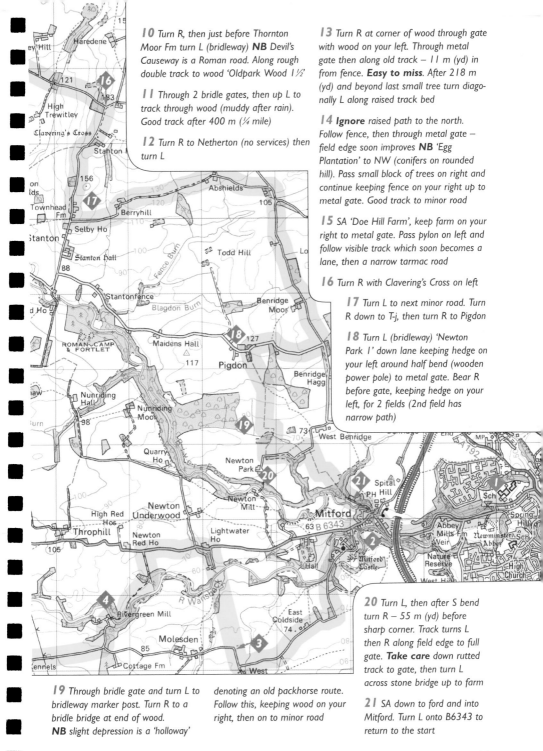

10 Turn R, then just before Thornton Moor Fm turn L (bridleway) **NB** Devil's Causeway is a Roman road. Along rough double track to wood 'Oldpark Wood 1½'

11 Through 2 bridle gates, then up L to track through wood (muddy after rain). Good track after 400 m (¼ mile)

12 Turn R to Netherton (no services) then turn L

13 Turn R at corner of wood through gate with wood on your left. Through metal gate then along old track – 11 m (yd) in from fence. **Easy to miss**. After 218 m (yd) and beyond last small tree turn diagonally L along raised track bed

14 Ignore raised path to the north. Follow fence, then through metal gate – field edge soon improves **NB** 'Egg Plantation' to NW (conifers on rounded hill). Pass small block of trees on right and continue keeping fence on your right up to metal gate. Good track to minor road

15 SA 'Doe Hill Farm', keep farm on your right to metal gate. Pass pylon on left and follow visible track which soon becomes a lane, then a narrow tarmac road

16 Turn R with Clavering's Cross on left

17 Turn L to next minor road. Turn R down to T-j, then turn R to Pigdon

18 Turn L (bridleway) 'Newton Park 1' down lane keeping hedge on your left around half bend (wooden power pole) to metal gate. Bear R before gate, keeping hedge on your left, for 2 fields (2nd field has narrow path)

19 Through bridle gate and turn L to bridleway marker post. Turn R to a bridle bridge at end of wood. **NB** slight depression is a 'holloway'

denoting an old packhorse route. Follow this, keeping wood on your right, then on to minor road

20 Turn L, then after S bend turn R – 55 m (yd) before sharp corner. Track turns L then R along field edge to full gate. **Take care** down rutted track to gate, then turn L across stone bridge up to farm

21 SA down to ford and into Mitford. Turn L onto B6343 to return to the start

6 The Rothbury Round

Rothbury is almost totally surrounded by heather-clad moors and wooded hills. Apart from one section of forest track, this long ride offers non-stop panoramic views of the route. Starting at Rothbury, the ride climbs steadily to Simonside Forest. The long descent into Harwood Forest is followed by a gentle gradient to a wonderful view-point, after which lies one of the most thrilling downhills in the UK! The short cut to Rothbury is via quiet minor roads and crosses the River Coquet beyond Newtown. If time and energy allow, then continue north and tackle the steady ascent to Wreighill and enjoy the subsequent descent to the level riverside fields. The route then uses undulating field paths and deserted, minor roads and, after a steady climb, the uniformally graded Carriage Drive (track). The ensuing descent into Rothbury is as memorable as it is steep. NB Contact Forest Enterprise (Rothbury 01669 620569) for free permit to cycle in Forest Enterprise forests.

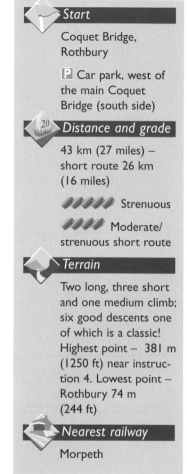

Start

Coquet Bridge, Rothbury

P Car park, west of the main Coquet Bridge (south side)

Distance and grade

43 km (27 miles) – short route 26 km (16 miles)

///// Strenuous

//// Moderate/ strenuous short route

Terrain

Two long, three short and one medium climb; six good descents one of which is a classic! Highest point – 381 m (1250 ft) near instruction 4. Lowest point – Rothbury 74 m (244 ft)

Nearest railway

Morpeth

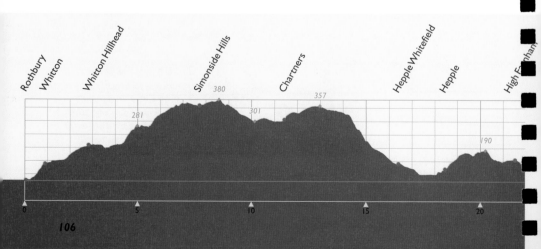

Cragside 1
A Victorian mansion built by the first Lord Armstrong in Wagnerian style – this showcase of Victorian art, architecture and technology is now a National Trust property. Set in 405 ha (1000 acres) of pine-covered hillside, lakes and tumbling streams, Cragside is especially famous for being the first (hydro) electrically powered house in the world. There are many other interesting features and remarkable inventions, too numerous to mention, all of which make Cragside a very special place

Holystone 8
Little more than a picturesque hamlet, Holystone offers an ideal *sojourn* on this major ride. The Salmon Inn has an old stone fireplace, behind which is a hidden cavity for hiding smuggled goods. Holystone boasts of two holy wells called St Mungo's and St Ninian's or the Lady's Well. Not far away, on Dove Crag Burn, lies Rob Roy's Cave

◀ Rothbury and Simonside Hills

Refreshments

The Sun tea room, pizzas, fish and chips, plenty of choice in **Rothbury** The Salmon Inn 🍴🍺, **Holystone** Cross Keys PH, Three Wheat Heads PH, **Thropton** (off-route)

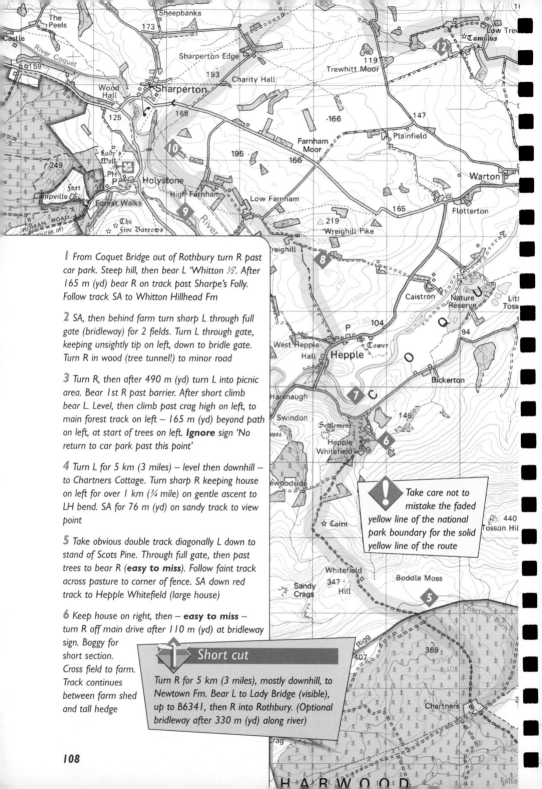

1 From Coquet Bridge out of Rothbury turn R past car park. Steep hill, then bear L 'Whitton ½'. After 165 m (yd) bear R on track past Sharpe's Folly. Follow track SA to Whitton Hillhead Fm

2 SA, then behind farm turn sharp L through full gate (bridleway) for 2 fields. Turn L through gate, keeping unsightly tip on left, down to bridle gate. Turn R in wood (tree tunnel!) to minor road

3 Turn R, then after 490 m (yd) turn L into picnic area. Bear 1st R past barrier. After short climb bear L. Level, then climb past crag high on left, to main forest track on left – 165 m (yd) beyond path on left, at start of trees on left. **Ignore** sign 'No return to car park past this point'

4 Turn L for 5 km (3 miles) – level then downhill – to Chartners Cottage. Turn sharp R keeping house on left for over 1 km (¾ mile) on gentle ascent to LH bend. SA for 76 m (yd) on sandy track to view point

5 Take obvious double track diagonally L down to stand of Scots Pine. Through full gate, then past trees to bear R (**easy to miss**). Follow faint track across pasture to corner of fence. SA down red track to Hepple Whitefield (large house)

6 Keep house on right, then – **easy to miss** – turn R off main drive after 110 m (yd) at bridleway sign. Boggy for short section. Cross field to farm. Track continues between farm shed and tall hedge

Take care not to mistake the faded yellow line of the national park boundary for the solid yellow line of the route

Short cut

Turn R for 5 km (3 miles), mostly downhill, to Newtown Fm. Bear L to Lady Bridge (visible), up to B6341, then R into Rothbury. (Optional bridleway after 330 m (yd) along river)

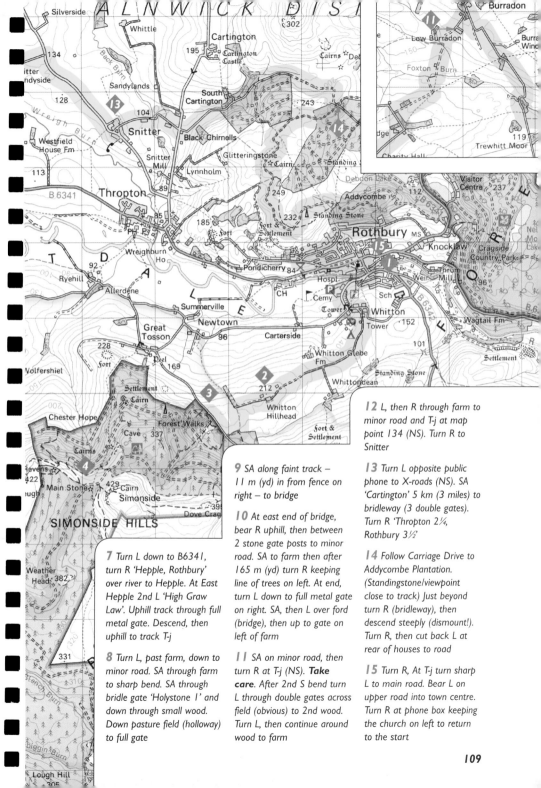

7 Turn L down to B6341, turn R 'Hepple, Rothbury' over river to Hepple. At East Hepple 2nd L 'High Graw Law'. Uphill track through full metal gate. Descend, then uphill to track T-j

8 Turn L, past farm, down to minor road. SA through farm to sharp bend. SA through bridle gate 'Holystone 1' and down through small wood. Down pasture field (holloway) to full gate

9 SA along faint track – 11 m (yd) in from fence on right – to bridge

10 At east end of bridge, bear R uphill, then between 2 stone gate posts to minor road. SA to farm then after 165 m (yd) turn R keeping line of trees on left. At end, turn L down to full metal gate on right. SA, then L over ford (bridge), then up to gate on left of farm

11 SA on minor road, then turn R at T-j (NS). **Take care**. After 2nd S bend turn L through double gates across field (obvious) to 2nd wood. Turn L, then continue around wood to farm

12 L, then R through farm to minor road and T-j at map point 134 (NS). Turn R to Snitter

13 Turn L opposite public phone to X-roads (NS). SA 'Cartington' 5 km (3 miles) to bridleway (3 double gates). Turn R 'Thropton 2¼, Rothbury 3½'

14 Follow Carriage Drive to Addycombe Plantation. (Standingstone/viewpoint close to track) Just beyond turn R (bridleway), then descend steeply (dismount!). Turn R, then cut back L at rear of houses to road

15 Turn R, At T-j turn sharp L to main road. Bear L on upper road into town centre. Turn R at phone box keeping the church on left to return to the start

South of Alnwick to the coast as far as Warkworth

Start

Outside of Alnwick just off the A1068 (GR 204125)

P Cross the A1, then turn down R into cul-de-sac

Distance and grade

43 km (27 miles) – short route 32 km (20 miles)

🖊 Easy

Terrain

Railway paths; edge of the sea bridleway; narrow lanes and green roads. Highest point – Freemans Hill 191 m (627 ft). Lowest point – sea level

Nearest railway

Alnmouth, just off the route near instructions 2/3

The Northumbrian coastline is one of the finest in Britain. It is clean, sandy, continuous and interspersed with cliffs, quiet bays, hidden coves and rocky headlands and there are long stretches of sand dunes. But that is not all; there are many old seaports and tiny harbours – each with their own small fishing fleet. Then, there are the castles of all sizes and states of repair and a diverse range of wildlife that the delicate coastline eco-structure supports. Cycling is an ideal way to enjoy the coast, provided the routes and their surfaces are sustainable; by the year 2000, Sustrans' Coast & Castles Route will connect Berwick-upon-Tweed with Tynemouth for such a route. This ride takes in an area of coastal hinterland in order to make a circuit possible. Beginning at Alnwick, and heading seaward by railway paths, UCRs and quiet lanes, the bridleway along the dunes south of Alnmouth is used to reach the attractive town of Warkworth with its imposing castle and quaint market place. The return to Alnwick utilises a similar combination of hitherto little-used byways and quiet lanes, which together make this ride a very enjoyable cycle tour.

The River Coquet approaching Warkworth

Close to yet another set of tight meanders with wooded cliffs stands Morwick Hall, formerly a property of the Grays of Howick. An old road passes by the Hall and goes down to one of two ancient fords, the lower one still known locally as Paupersford. When the river was safe to ford, the grass lane that leads up to instruction 7 would have been the continuation route. When riding section 6, look out for the raised 'road' base that runs parallel to the hedge and meets this bridleway at right angles. From this traverse, a tall sandstone cliff catches the eye, on it are several ancient 'cup and ring' markings the purpose of which are not fully understood. These also occur elsewhere in Northumberland but none so close to sea level

▼ Alnmouth

Refreshments

Plenty of choice in **Alnwick**
Plenty of choice in **Warkworth**
The Cook and Barker Inn PH, **Newton on the Moor**
(off the route, via minor roads with dangerous A1 crossing)

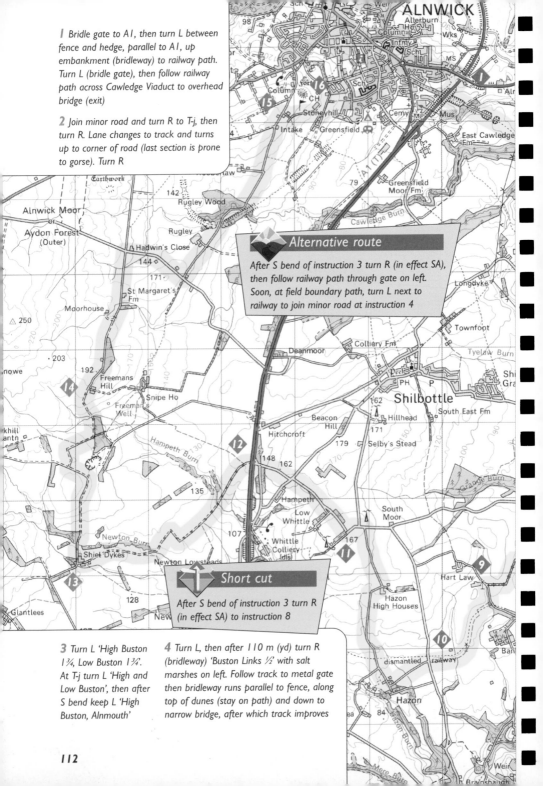

1 Bridle gate to A1, then turn L between fence and hedge, parallel to A1, up embankment (bridleway) to railway path. Turn L (bridle gate), then follow railway path across Cawledge Viaduct to overhead bridge (exit)

2 Join minor road and turn R to T-j, then turn R. Lane changes to track and turns up to corner of road (last section is prone to gorse). Turn R

Alternative route

After S bend of instruction 3 turn R (in effect SA), then follow railway path through gate on left. Soon, at field boundary path, turn L next to railway to join minor road at instruction 4

Short cut

After S bend of instruction 3 turn R (in effect SA) to instruction 8

3 Turn L 'High Buston 1¾, Low Buston 1¾'. At T-j turn L 'High and Low Buston', then after S bend keep L 'High Buston, Alnmouth'

4 Turn L, then after 110 m (yd) turn R (bridleway) 'Buston Links ½' with salt marshes on left. Follow track to metal gate then bridleway runs parallel to fence, along top of dunes (stay on path) and down to narrow bridge, after which track improves

5 SA past caravans to A1068 and turn L into Warkworth. SA up to castle, passing it on your right, then SA

6 Turn R at Waters Haugh Road, then after 55 m (yd) turn sharp L (NS) down to ford (bridge for high water). Pass caravan site then SA (when road bears right) through double set of gates. Keep high, with hedge on right, to wood, then turn R (bridleway). (**For** river picnic turn L then retrace)

7 Turn L over bridge then turn R 'Brotherwick ¾, Warkworth 2¾'. At T-j turn L 'Shilbottle 2½'

8 Turn L 'Sturton Grange ¼, South Moor 1' then after 656 m (yd) turn L 'Southside' to and then around farm. Lane changes to a good track

9 Turn L, then – **easy to miss** – after 275 m (yd) cut back R on concealed railway path (bridleway), Look for set-back gate on right, path is hidden behind overgrown earth mound; do not pass under single overhead cable which crosses the minor road **beyond** the bridleway

10 **NB** railway path can be narrow. Turn L, then sharp R to turn R at Hazon

11 Turn L, then again after 110 m (yd) in effect SA to sharp corner, then to off-set T-j. Turn L then immediately R (NS) to A1

12 **Take care**. Cross A1 at right angles. Through gate opposite (NS) but between 2 Clearway cancel signs. Follow track SA to Shiel Dykes Fm

13 Turn R up to old quarry; track curves L, then – **easy to miss** – after 330 m (yd) turn R, turns R to wood then L up to farm

14 SA down to T-j, then turn R for short sharp climb to next T-j. Turn L to Intake

15 Just before Golf Course turn R (bridleway) 'Swansfield Park ¾', then turn L across short section of the course to track then narrow tarmac road. Turn R down to bend and bear L

16 Turn R down bridleway to estate road. SA to T-j, then turn L. Turn R at PO to A1068. Turn R to round-about, then fork L to start

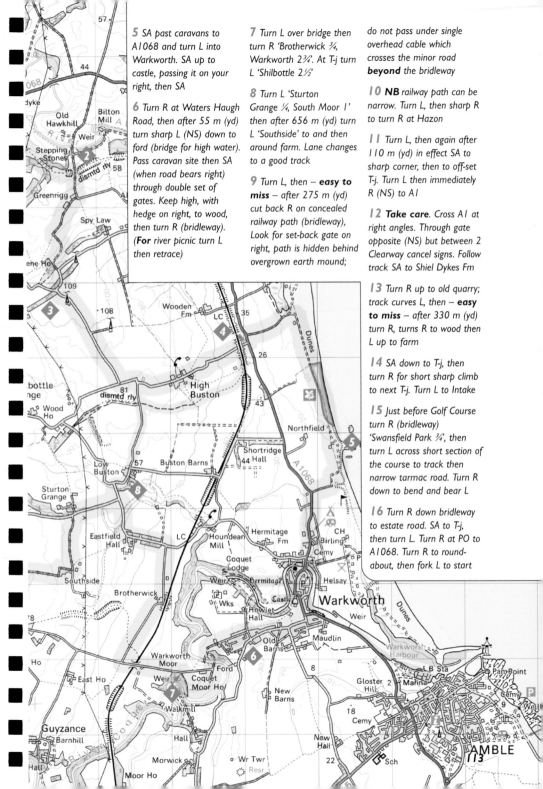

East of Alnwick to the coast, north to Craster

This ride has the benefit of including a reasonable length of coastal cycling, part of the Sustrans' Coast & Castles Route. The River Aln is forded (once wet, the already tricky stepping stones are lethal) Then it is down to Alnmouth before an unavoidable on-road stretch to Boulmer and the start of a first class cliff-top track to Sea Houses. There is a short on-road link up to a contrasting rural section, then it is down the road to Craster with its tiny harbour and seaside cottages. Looping back through Dunstan, two almost-connecting off-road sections lead through the sleepy village of Rennington to 4 km (2½ miles) of UCR leaving a little over 2 km (1¼ miles) of relatively quiet B road, which gently slopes back to the start.

Start

Next to B1340, north of Alnwick, before slip road to A1
(GR 200143)

P As above

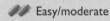

Distance and grade

34 km (21 miles) – short route 32 km (20 miles)

Easy/moderate

Easy

Terrain

Green roads, quiet lanes and bridleways – mostly level. Highest point – between instructions 14/15 104 m (344 ft). Lowest point – sea level

Nearest railway

Alnmouth, on the route

Refreshments

Plenty of choice in **Alnwick**
Plenty of choice in **Alnmouth**
Jolly Fisherman PH, Bark Pots tea room, shop and restaurant, **Craster**
Cottage Inn PH, **Dunstan**
Horse Shoes Inn PH, **Rennington**

The coast

Boulmer lifeboat station stands next to the road and is indicative of the skill and courage that this important service exemplifies. There are always a number of cobles nearby; these are Northumbrian fishing boats based on an original design concept borrowed from the Viking long boats that allows the boats to be launched from the beach and still be very stable on the sea in all conditions. Note the guide posts in the bay, which indicate a safe channel for the boats. Houdiemont Sands and Sugar Sands are two lovely beaches as is Howick Haven; Rumbling Kern is a cave that causes the sea to growl when it swells into it at certain tide levels and strengths, colloquially called a 'woofy hole', which is onomatopoeic!

▼ *Craster*

Howick Hall · Dunstan · Littlemill · Rennington · Broxfield · Denwick Lane End

47

20 · 25 · 30 · 33.8

105

0

1 Cross A1, then turn R at Denwick church, tarmac changes to track (Rabbit Lonnen) **NB** 'Lonnen' means a lane. At A1068 turn L, then next R at X-roads to river – **take care** – stepping stones are very slippery and uneven, do not attempt to cross if they are submerged!

2 Up to Greenrigg Fm, turn left to Bilton. Turn L to Hipsburn roundabout then SA to Alnmouth roundabout. Turn R for Main Street and at far end turn L to loop back to instruction 3

3 SA keeping church on your L to fork, then turn R to Boulmer – a necessary on-road section

4 SA at sharp corner (2 cul-de-sac signs) along cliff track for 3 km (2 miles) and enjoy this fine coastal path

5 Turn L to Howick Hall entrance

6 Turn R past wall on your left, then SA to follow high deer fence on your left, through gate with mature wood on your left to far end. Turn L through gate on your left (**ignore** gate SA into open field), then after 11 m (yd), almost into next field, bear R – **easy to miss** – along narrow path through narrow belt of mature trees

7 Turn L on good track for 220 m (yd) then at bend turn R along field edge keeping plantation on your right (2 fields). Cross small bridge, then through bridle gate and turn L along field edge to corner of field. Turn R along field edge to road

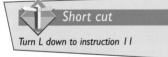

Short cut

Turn L down to instruction 11

8 Turn R to X-roads.
Turn L to Dunstan (PH) then bear L to next bend in road (**Or** SA to Craster/Dunstanburgh Castle then retrace to Dunstan Village)

9 Through bridle gate, past old hemmel (stone, cattle building), follow edge of field (bridleway) keeping wood and fence on your left, to next wood. Through gate, then turn L down tree avenue. Next section to bridle gate is uneven due to horse use and muddy when wet – walk if necessary

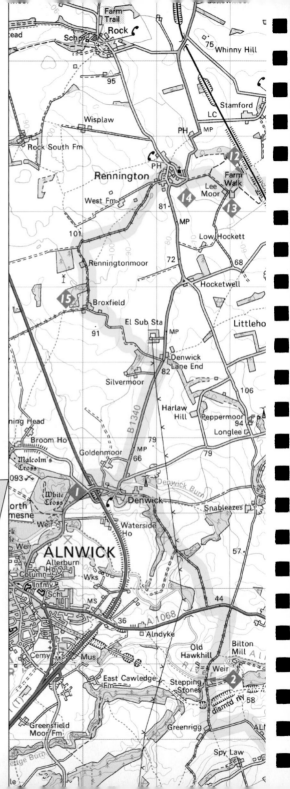

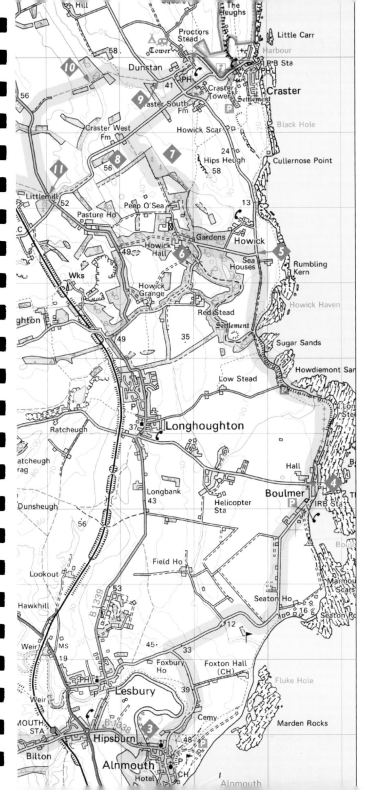

10 SA along field edge keeping fence and both blocks of trees on your left, through gate, then SA on obvious double track to minor road. Turn L

11 Turn R (field gate some 110 m (110 yd) NW of small bridge before X-roads) and follow field edge next to fence on your right. Through tunnel, then turn R (best line is some 11 m (yd) in from railway fence)

12 **Easy to miss.** Turn L to bridle gate (between 4th/5th railway pylons from tunnel and some 130 m (yd) before single wooden electric power pole in field). Cross small bridge. **NB** Conservation notice through gate on left. You are now on a Countryside Access farm; SA with fence on your left

13 Turn R at farm and cross open area. SA passing cottages on your left (sign 'Farm Walk' – please show considera-tion). Through end gate, then bear L towards church keeping hedge on your left

14 Turn R, then L (in effect SA) 'Rock 1¼' into Rennington (PH). Turn L, then turn R at end of village green at farm. After 220 m (yd), at end of cottages, fork L

15 **Take care.** Through farm, then turn L to B1340 and turn R to return to the start

9 A super circuit on scenic byways, south of Wooler

The rolling Cheviot Hills are full of wild places (they have an indigenous herd of wild goats) and it is not difficult to feel lonely when cycling or walking in their midst – or even in their mist! This ride comes within gasping distance of these wonderful hills and through proximity provides a taste of what they have to offer the committed off-road cyclist. Our route heads south of Wooler along narrow, minor roads and old byways that were once the area's main thoroughfares. After several enjoyable undulations, the rewarding descent into Roseden is capped with a high-quality refreshment opportunity before the route swings very pleasantly eastwards towards Old Bewick. The ascent and subsequent cross-fell section take you to the aptly named Blawearie. A surprisingly acceptable fell track links with the magnificent Hepburn Moor road, and with the further use of quiet lanes and green roads the return route to Wooler maintains its interest and charm with more bountiful views of the Cheviots.

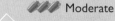 **Start**

High Street, Wooler

P Padgepool Place to the west of Wooler High Street

Distance and grade

34 km (21 miles) – short route 19 km (12 miles)

 Moderate

Terrain

Descents seem to outweigh the ascents over this mixed terrain route. The Hepburn downhill is amazing but needs control and traffic awareness. Highest point – fell approaching instruction 7 253 m (830 ft). Lowest point – near Wooler 52 m (172 ft)

Nearest railway

Berwick-upon-Tweed, 27 km (17 miles) north of Wooler

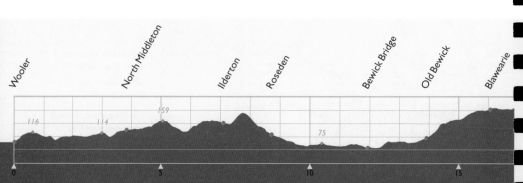

Wooler 1

Wooler means 'hill overlooking a stream' and makes the ideal base for an extended visit to this area and one that gives easy access to the Cheviot Hills. Situated on a small plateau and its approach slopes, the small market town of Wooler overlooks the Wooler Water. Passing by such evocative places as Scald Hill, Skirl Naked and Happy Valley, the Wooler Water is then deflected northwards to its confluence with the River Till, which then kinks its way north westwards with the sole purpose of emptying its contents into the River Tweed

The Cheviot Hills

The Cheviot Hills stretch for about 35 km (22 miles) along the northwest border of Northumberland and being some 34 km (21 miles) wide, the total area of rolling, grassy and heather-clad hills, of which about one third lies in Scotland, amounts to over 480 km^2 (300 miles^2) of wonderful scenery

The Bewicks

Bewick means 'bee farm', which bears testimony to the fact that the neighbouring moors are a reliable source of honey. In times gone by, this was of great significance before imported sugar became available and honey was virtually the only source of available sweetening and beeswax was used in great quantities both in the home and in churches. The left turn to tiny Old Bewick church, next to the Kirk Burn, is marked by an inscribed Saxon cross and is well worth the slight detour – it is said to have been built by Queen Maud, wife of Henry I. Ancient earthworks abound as do cup and ring marked rocks. En route to Blawearie an old wagonway lies next to several holloways, where rock has been chiselled to permit wheeled passage

Refreshments

Plenty of choice in **Wooler**
Tea room, restaurant and shop,
Roseden Farm

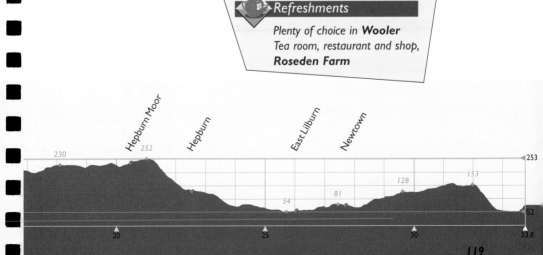

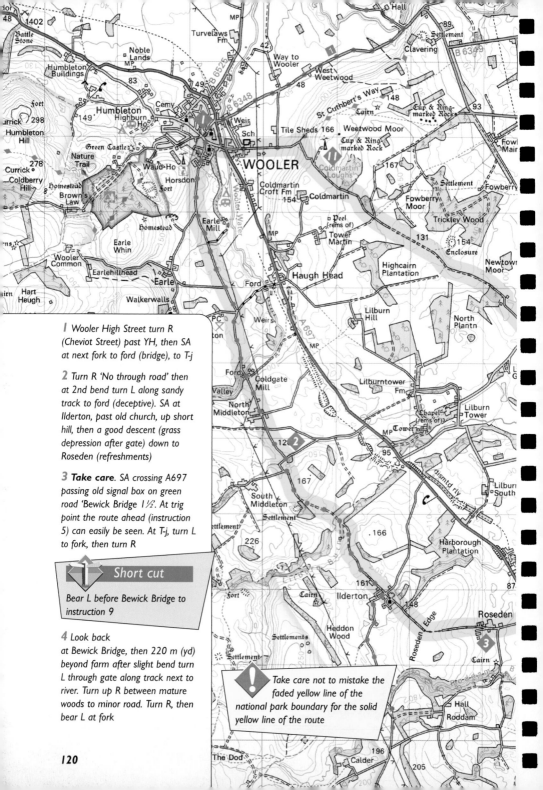

1 Wooler High Street turn R (Cheviot Street) past YH, then SA at next fork to ford (bridge), to T-j

2 Turn R 'No through road' then at 2nd bend turn L along sandy track to ford (deceptive). SA at Ilderton, past old church, up short hill, then a good descent (grass depression after gate) down to Roseden (refreshments)

3 *Take care*. SA crossing A697 passing old signal box on green road 'Bewick Bridge 1½'. At trig point the route ahead (instruction 5) can easily be seen. At T-j, turn L to fork, then turn R

Short cut

Bear L before Bewick Bridge to instruction 9

4 Look back at Bewick Bridge, then 220 m (yd) beyond farm after slight bend turn L through gate along track next to river. Turn up R between mature woods to minor road. Turn R, then bear L at fork

! Take care not to mistake the faded yellow line of the national park boundary for the solid yellow line of the route

5 Turn L at farm and follow track ahead up to fell. Through metal gate, then bear L to distant gate. Track reduces up to Blawearie. **Warning** – do not continue in bad visibility or inclement weather. (Navigation aid: if visible/after Blawearie – head to distant mast on right)

6 Stay a while to enjoy this wonderful place! Follow track behind and beyond Blawearie, short climb before descent to track T-j 33 m (yd) in front of sheep cabin. Turn R across seemingly open fell and follow track close to holloways. Look for a marker post, a hurdle gate close to small stream, 2 further marker posts then track improves to road

7 Turn L across moor (narrow road), then descend carefully down 1:8 hill (exceptional views) to T-j. SA down grass lane. **Warning** – do not attempt instruction 8 if the river is likely to be full. If uncertain, advance inspection is recommended (short detour before instruction 4)

8 Turn L down to river (footbridge unusable) which can be crossed by stepping-stones (homemade) or paddling (through hurdle on R, then across to shingle shore), then on to minor road

Chillingham Castle

Turn R to Chillingham Castle gates, then turn L to Newtown T-j. Turn R to continue with instruction 10

9 Turn R to farm T-j and turn R over ford (bridge) to Newtown T-j

10 Bear L to wide junction then SA 'West Lilburn'. Lane changes to track, keep SA

11 Track changes to tarmac lane, descend steeply – **take care** – to cross A697 and up the short, sharp sting in the tail to return to the start

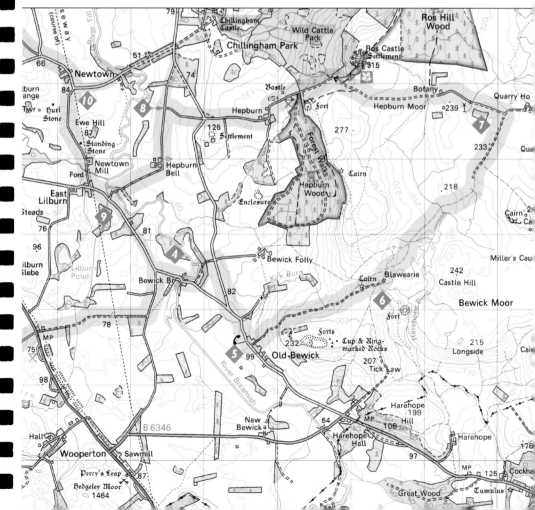

West of Belford to St Cuthbert's Cave and Ravens Crag

10

*T*his ride is recommended for its special qualities; take a generous measure of situation and add incredible views on all sides, plenty of history and atmosphere with wildlife habitats and wetlands, add some favourable gradients and this ride is the result! Starting at Belford, what was possibly an old thoroughfare or through route, heads northwest past a variety of interesting locations, to the Swinhoe road. Passing the old continuation road on the right, an excellent track slopes up gently to Dick's Oldwalls and then girdles the hill past eye-catching Cockenheugh and the splendid St Cuthbert's Cave. After traversing close to Holburn Farm, a short climb curves round Raven's Crag and past Holburn Moss to descend pleasantly to Detchant. The A1 crossing needs great care and after a short woodland thrash, the return route loops back to Belford by a quiet, minor road that only becomes busier in the final 2 km (1¼ miles). Choose a fine day and enjoy this lovely circuit – it may be short but it contains more than its fair share of magic.

 Start

Main Street, Belford

P On B6349 west end of Belford

 Distance and grade

21 km (13 miles) – short route 18 km (11 miles)

✐ Easy

 Terrain

Despite the reasonable brevity of this route, it contains within it a wide range of ground surfaces, although principally the route follows good tracks. Some sections can be muddy after rain or overgrown in midsummer. Highest point – Holburn Moss 160 m (525 ft). Lowest point – near Elwick 5 m (17 ft)

 Nearest railway

Berwick-upon-Tweed, 24 km (15 miles) north of the start

Belford   Swinhoe Farm   156   147   Raven's Crag   151

95

0   5   10

St Cuthbert's Cave 5

This remarkable natural sandstone cave is where, it is thought, the saint's body rested for a short time on its way to Durham. In 1833, a medieval ring was found in this cave, one of a number of such finds in the locality. A visit in springtime is rewarded with an avenue of daffodils that lead the eye down through the wider avenue of pines to where the not-so-distant Cheviot Hills are perfectly framed

Holburn Moss 6

Holburn Moss is one of only two Ramsar sites in the North East of England, the other being on Holy Island; representing over 90 countries, the Ramsar Convention, named after the town in Iran, exists to conserve important wetland sites

Smeafield 9

Originally Smith's Field, but the type of field all depends on the date of the name; prior to the Black Death in 1348, the word 'feld' meant an open space or expanse larger than a clearing as in Flodden Field. Land enclosure after the Black Death saw the gradual adoption of 'field' as we now know it

◄ St. Cuthbert's Cave near Belford in Glendale

1 W from Main Street on B6349, turn R at Community Club (bridleway) to Westhall Fm, then turn R at steading to Craggyhall Fm. SA past old limekiln to gate. Follow field-edge path to bridle gate

2 Through gate into wood (permissive path) to track T-j (white house ahead). Turn L to minor road, then SA to Swinhoe Fm

Short cut

Just before farm, turn R through belt of trees, through gate and along raised field-edge path (fence on right) to gate. Through gate, turn R and follow improving track to minor road

3 SA past farm on wide track past Dick Oldwalls (disused building) and on to trees (coastal views to rear)

4 SA, then track bears R and with trees only on your right, good views of the Cheviots. Look for Cockenheugh rock towers on your R followed by St Cuthbert's Cave on your R near end of wood

5 SA to contour hillside and on to lane east of Holburn Fm. Look out for field edge dogs leg L, then R 400 m (¼ mile) before farm track

6 Turn R, then uphill to circuit between Raven's Crag and Rabbit Hill re-entering trees. Follow obvious track out of trees, around and down, to Greymare Fm

7 SA by farm to minor road, then down to Detchant (short-cut track comes in from right). SA to Detchant Lodge

8 **Take great care**. SA on track to cross A1, then SA over railway line into belt of tall trees down to cross small bridge. Track then turns R up to minor road (long grass in Summer)

9 Turn R, then at obvious fork bear R

10 Turn R, then over LC on busier road. Cross A1 – **take care** – using offset tarmac footpaths for increased safety then SA back to Start

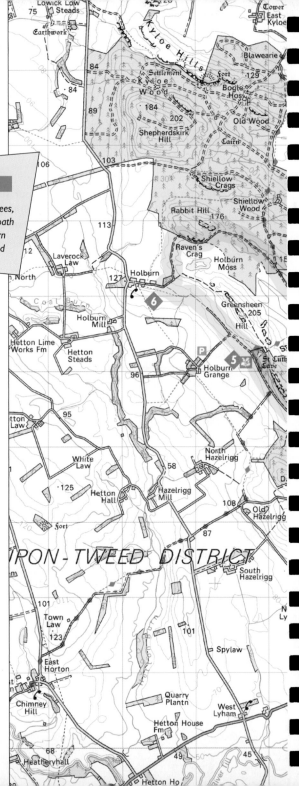

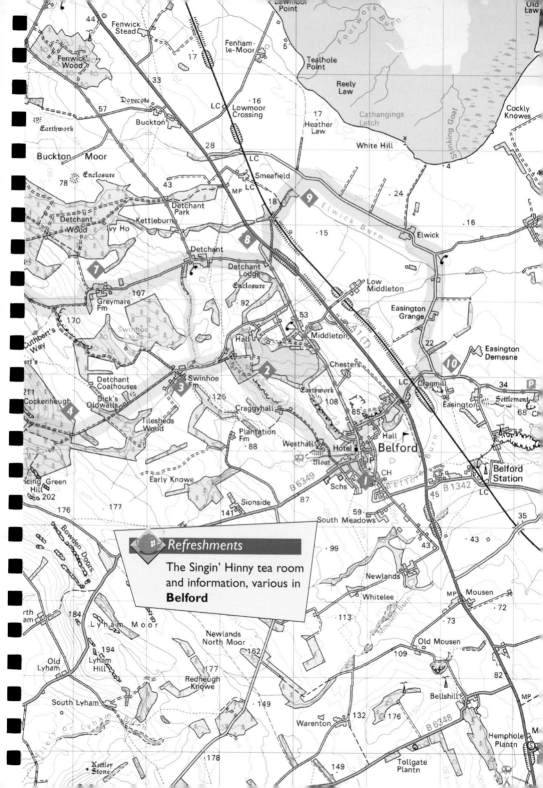

Refreshments

The Singin' Hinny tea room and information, various in **Belford**

Notes

Notes

Useful addresses

British Cycling Federation
National Cycling Centre
Stuart Street
Manchester M11 4DQ
0870 871 2000
www.bcf.uk.com

The BCF co-ordinates and promotes an array of cycle sports and cycling in general. They are a good first point of contact if you want to find out more about how to get involved in cycling. The website provides information on upcoming cycle events and competitions.

CTC (Cyclists Touring Club)
Cotterell House
69 Meadrow
Godalming
Surrey GU7 3HS
01483 417217
www.ctc.org.uk

Britain's largest cycling organisation, promoting recreational and utility cycling. The CTC provides touring and technical advice, legal aid and insurance, and campaigns to improve facilities and opportunities for all cyclists. The website provides details of campaigns and routes and has an online application form.

The London Cycling Campaign
Unit 228
30 Great Guildford Street
London SE1 0HS
020 7928 7220
www.lcc.org.uk

The LCC promotes cycling in London by providing services for cyclists and by campaigning for more facilities for cyclists. Membership of the LCC provides the following benefits: London Cyclist magazine, insurance, legal advice, workshops, organised rides, discounts in bike shops and much more. You can join the LCC on its website.

Sustrans
Head Office
Crown House
37-41 Prince Street
Bristol BS1 4PS
General information line: 0117 929 0888
www.sustrans.org.uk

A registered charity, Sustrans designs and builds systems for sustainable transport. It is best known for its transformation of old railway lines into safe, traffic-free routes for cyclists and pedestrians and wheelchair users. Sustrans is developing the 13,000 km (8000 mile) National Cycle Network on traffic-calmed minor roads and traffic-free paths, to be completed by the year 2005 with major funding from the Millennium Commission.

Veteran Cycle Club
Membership Secretary
31 Yorke Road
Croxley Green
Rickmansworth
Herts WD3 3DW
www.v-cc.org.uk

A very active club, the VCC is concerned with the history and restoration of veteran cycles. Members enjoy organised rides and receive excellent publications relating to cycle history and club news.